# THE ART OF
# CHANGE

# THE ART OF
# CHANGE

## Transforming Paradoxes into Breakthroughs

## JEFF DEGRAFF
## AND STANEY DEGRAFF

**BK·**

Berrett–Koehler Publishers, Inc.

Berrett-Koehler Publishers, Inc.
1333 Broadway, Suite P100
Oakland, CA 94612-1921
Tel: (510) 817-2277
Fax: (510) 817-2278
bkconnection.com

ORDERING INFORMATION

**Quantity sales.** Special discounts are available on quantity purchases by corporations, associations, and others. For details, please go to bkconnection.com to see our bulk discounts or contact bookorders@bkpub.com for more information.
**Individual sales.** Berrett-Koehler publications are available through most bookstores. They can also be ordered directly from Berrett-Koehler: Tel: (800) 929-2929; Fax: (802) 864-7626; bkconnection.com.
**Orders for college textbook / course adoption use.** Please contact Berrett-Koehler: Tel: (800) 929-2929; Fax: (802) 864-7626.

Distributed to the US trade and internationally by Penguin Random House Publisher Services.
The authorized representative in the EU for product safety and compliance is EU Compliance Partner, Pärnu mnt. 139b-14, 11317 Tallinn, Estonia, www.eucompliancepartner.com, +372 5368 65 02

Berrett-Koehler and the BK logo are registered trademarks of Berrett-Koehler Publishers, Inc.

Printed in Canada

Berrett-Koehler books are printed on long-lasting acid-free paper. When it is available, we choose paper that has been manufactured by environmentally responsible processes. These may include using trees grown in sustainable forests, incorporating recycled paper, minimizing chlorine in bleaching, or recycling the energy produced at the paper mill.

Library of Congress Cataloging-in-Publication Data

Names: DeGraff, Jeffrey Thomas, author. | DeGraff, Staney, author.
Title: The art of change : transforming paradoxes into breakthroughs / Jeff DeGraff, Staney DeGraff.
Description: First edition. | Oakland, CA : Berrett-Koehler Publishers, Inc., [2025] | Includes bibliographical references and index.
Identifiers: LCCN 2024044537 (print) | LCCN 2024044538 (ebook) | ISBN 9798890570680 (paperback) | ISBN 9798890570697 (pdf) | ISBN 9798890570703 (epub)
Subjects: LCSH: Self-actualization (Psychology) | Change (Psychology) | Leadership.
Classification: LCC BF637.S4 D4347 2025 (print) | LCC BF637.S4 (ebook) | DDC 158.1—dc23/eng/20250115
LC record available at https://lccn.loc.gov/2024044537
LC ebook record available at https://lccn.loc.gov/2024044538

First Edition

33 32 31 30 29 28 27 26 25    10 9 8 7 6 5 4 3 2 1

Book production: 1000 Books / Susan Geraghty
Cover design: Rob Johnson

This book is dedicated to Robert E. Quinn and
Kim S. Cameron, our friends and mentors,
who led the way with blazing light.

Also to our editor, Steve Piersanti,
whose insights bring wisdom.

This is for all the
Changemakers in the world.

# CONTENTS

# PREFACE

THIS BOOK IS DEDICATED TO you, the leaders navigating the complexities of transformation in your professional and personal lives. Change is endless, and mastering it is a lifelong journey. True transformation begins within. By first changing ourselves as individuals and leaders, we unlock the potential to transform our teams and organizations. Through your personal growth, you can inspire a thriving organizational culture, elevate competencies, and foster a vibrant community. As visionary leaders, you embody the culture, practices, and competencies you aspire to see. In essence, you lead by example, guiding those around you to embrace and champion change.

We often find ourselves at crossroads that feel both daunting and full of potential, asking, "What now?" Whether facing personal changes or monumental societal shifts like the rise of artificial intelligence, the common thread is the journey through uncertainty.

This book reflects over forty years of advising and nurturing change across various sectors—from the most innovative tech companies to large multinational conglomerates, distinguished military organizations, revered academic institutions, and celebrated cultural establishments. We have witnessed firsthand the birth and growth of groundbreaking innovation ecosystems that have thrived and become dynastic in their reach and influence. Although change processes differ for a start-up versus a large conglomerate, underlying truths span all industries and sizes. These truths are the threads we pull and magnify for you to see.

Gone are the days when one-size-fits-all solutions or neat checklists sufficed to manage the complexities of change. Our world demands a nuanced approach—one that embraces adaptability. This adaptability, or the paradoxical mindset, is central to the thesis of this book. It's about more than just coping; it's about thriving amid the flux, utilizing our inherent capacity to evolve both thoughts and actions in real time.

This work encourages you to introspect deeply, questioning not just the external "whats" and "hows" but the internal "whys" and "whos." It is about understanding who you are, recognizing your genuine capabilities and limitations, and applying this understanding to navigate life's complexities. This work insists on reflective practice, in which every experience is a lesson and every setback a setup for a comeback.

Yet how do you move toward a destination that is unclear or unknown? How do you deal with ambiguous and rapidly changing situations? The answer lies in developing a new way of thinking—a new mindset that embraces ambiguity and helps you grow. This mindset is adaptive, flexible, and agile and can be developed through understanding competing elements, namely *paradoxes*. Merriam-Webster (n.d.) defines a paradox as "a statement that is seemingly contradictory or opposed to common sense and yet is perhaps true." Howard Alexander Slaatte, a Methodist minister and professor of philosophy, offers a more descriptive definition in his book *The Pertinence of the Paradox*:

> A paradox is an idea involving two opposite thoughts or propositions, which, however contradictory, are equally necessary to convey a more imposing, illuminating, life-related or provocative insight into truth than either factor can muster in its own right. What the mind seemingly cannot think it must think; what reason is reluctant to express it must express. (Slaatte, 1968, as cited in Cameron, 1986, p. 545)

*The Art of Change* helps you embrace the power of paradoxes and use them as catalysts for growth and transformation. It does not promise easy answers; instead, it equips you with the mindset to recognize and leverage the opportunities that lie within challenges.

This book is written for three distinct audiences: leaders involved in a change effort, leaders who want to improve their leadership skills, and individuals who seek to transform their own lives, as well as those of their friends and family. It provides valuable insights and practical strategies tailored to each group, addressing the complexities of leading and managing change in organizational contexts, enhancing personal leadership capabilities, and fostering individual growth and transformation. Whether you are spearheading a major organizational initiative, striving to improve your leadership effectiveness, or embarking on a personal journey of self-improvement, *The Art of Change* offers the guidance and tools needed to navigate and thrive in an ever-evolving landscape.

Enriched by the voices of renowned thought leaders and innovators, this book offers strategies, tools, and insights to help you forge your path. These resources are drawn not from hypothetical scenarios but from real-world applications and proven successes. They aim to guide, inspire, and provoke thought, urging you to mold an innovative future.

As you turn each page, remember that you are a work in progress, as are the solutions and strategies you will encounter. This book is an invitation to move forward—onward and ever upward—in your continual quest for growth and excellence. Let it be a companion and a guide as you navigate the evolving landscapes of your life and work.

Embrace this journey with openness and curiosity. Let each chapter challenge you to adapt, transform, and ultimately transcend the complexities of your context. This is not just a book; it is a tool for transformation—yours and that of the worlds you influence.

# Introduction
## Inviting Paradox In

L UIS, A DISTINGUISHED COLONEL WITH a strategic mindset, faced a critical challenge that threatened national preparedness: the sluggish pace at which the military acquired new technologies. In an era when technological advancements were pivotal for strategic geopolitical stability, this delay was not only a procedural inconvenience but a significant threat to national security. Luis recognized that the existing acquisition process, deeply entrenched in bureaucratic red tape, was not just slow but dangerously outdated in a rapidly evolving technological landscape. His vision—to create an alternative, more efficient pathway for adopting breakthrough innovations—was born out of this urgent need for change.

Feeling the weight of responsibility on his shoulders, Luis began assembling an unconventional team. This group did not comprise traditional soldiers but a diverse mix of minds: Pentagon officials who understood the intricacies of military bureaucracy, academics with fresh perspectives, leaders from cutting-edge tech companies, and experienced acquisition officers from various military bases. Each member had personally witnessed how the current system stifled innovation, hindering both technological advancement and those who championed it. Together, they were poised to tackle this daunting task, aiming to revolutionize the military's approach to technological adoption, a move critical for maintaining national security in an age of rapid and unpredictable change.

At the onset of winter, guided by the authors, Jeff and Staney, they met for a week in a simple, unassuming room in Ann Arbor, a space more suited to start-ups than the military. The key conflict within Luis's team stemmed from the clash of different professional cultures and priorities. Pentagon officials, accustomed to strict military protocols and cautious decision-making, often conflicted with tech company leaders who advocated for rapid innovation and agility. Meanwhile, academics, with their focus on theoretical and long-term implications, found themselves at odds with acquisition officers, who were grounded in the practicalities and immediate needs of military operations. These tensions highlighted the fundamental challenge in harmonizing diverse approaches to revolutionize the military's technology acquisition process. Ideas clashed and egos were bruised, but out of that creative friction came something remarkable. The team devised a streamlined acquisition process, lean and effective. It was an outsider's solution to an insider's problem, cutting through the red tape that had ensnarled them all for so long.

Then the COVID pandemic hit. Suddenly, the world was in chaos, and the federal government turned to the military to lead the effort to distribute the vaccines as quickly and widely as possible. Luis's new acquisition process, initially designed for a different purpose, proved invaluable. It was used to procure billions of vials and needles necessary to deliver the vaccine, a complex array of cold-storage facilities to preserve the vaccine, and a network of health care professionals to administer injections to millions of people. His system was agile, quick, and everything the old system wasn't. And it worked.

For a brief moment, Luis was celebrated and heralded as a visionary, but organizations have short and selective memories. Deviating from the prescribed career pathway to advancement was perilous, and in a system where you move up or out, the functionaries thanked him for his service and showed him the door. Though his acquisition process survived the change, Luis did not. He had disrupted the status quo, and the system pushed back.

The story of Luis could be your own story. Perhaps you're a change-maker, driven by a profound dissatisfaction with the status quo. You come across as negative, but in reality, you harbor a very positive belief that things can be better. You have good ideas on how to transform your organization, but you have trouble selling them, and even bigger challenges trying to get them implemented effectively.

To make change happen, you must first recognize the paradox of the transformational leader—organizations love change, but hate their changemakers. Changemakers are often undermined, then pushed out, even when their change initiatives succeed. This is not personal. Effective leaders understand how their organizations work and don't work. Yet ironically, that's why we, the changemakers, who work for and with effective leaders, take it personally. The structure and dynamics of organizations are designed to maintain their equilibrium. Organizations are built to eliminate as much variance as feasible. Change, by definition, is a form of deviance or difference. Changemakers need to understand this and therefore start their change efforts by changing their own mindset.

## It's All in Your Mind

This pandemic experience reminded us, the authors, to ask some fundamental questions about change management. Ancient historians from Herodotus to Thucydides, and historians throughout the ages, have written about the inevitability of pandemics, wars, political upheavals, natural disasters, and financial collapses, so why are we, as a species, frequently unprepared for them? And once they occur, why are we so bad at adjusting to the changing circumstances? Most important, why can't most leaders adapt effectively to meet these challenges in real time before those challenges become a full-blown crisis?

As illustrated in Luis's story, our inadvertent role in facilitating a rapid response underscored a fundamental issue: the prevalent focus on rigid structures and predetermined goals in leadership training. Traditionally, change management has often been treated as an offshoot of project management. Leaders establish fixed targets and employ streamlined processes to reach those objectives. However, true mastery of change requires a different approach, one that prioritizes time as a critical factor, given the inherently ambiguous and ever-evolving nature of crises.

Consider the early days of the pandemic when knowledge of the COVID virus was limited. The world's initial responses were inevitably inaccurate and ineffective because scientists lacked sufficient information about its genome and how it spread. As time passed, our collective understanding improved, and our ability to develop effective solutions grew with each new insight.

Bureaucracies are necessary to manage large and complex organizational systems. They provide stability and predictability. Change will always attract opposition from them because it brings instability. The paradoxes of change in large organizational systems are striking: these bureaucracies are designed to create standardization and thereby favor stability and predictability by minimizing all that deviates from the norm. As such, bureaucracies inherently work against the change and adaptation required for growth and relevance in a dynamic environment. This means that those of us who would steer change need to both embrace and reject the reliability of existing systems.

It's not just that change introduces something new; it's that it ideally will end something old. When someone believes they are protecting something sacred, they are far more likely to resist a change. To excel in change management, leaders and organizations must develop a high tolerance for ambiguity, a paradoxical mindset, and the courage to explore unconventional solutions. In short, to expect the unexpected.

## The Fluidity of Time

How do you get somewhere that you've never been before when you don't know the way and you aren't even sure the place really exists? How confident would you be in your plans? Do you have the right crew, vehicle, route, and provisions? When you aren't sure where you're going or how to get there, you hedge and diversify your plans. You plan to make stops along the way, get information from other travelers, and course-correct as needed. In essence, change is like a voyage of discovery, replete with perilous threats. Journeying across this unbounded ocean, where the familiar contours of the present are continually molded by the relentless forces of time and circumstance, the less you are committed to your approach, the more likely you are to survive. At its heart, this journey involves a profound realization—that change, in all its multi-faceted forms, is not an external event to be managed but rather an intrinsic facet of the human experience.

Change hinges on an acute awareness of timing—an ability to navigate and adapt to the ever-unfolding rhythms and cadences of the dynamic changes that surround us. Synchronization with time's inexorable flow is imminently elusive, but even attempting alignment pushes us to develop alternative strategies for effectively managing change.

Throughout history, thinkers spanning from Heraclitus, who mused about the ever-changing river, to more contemporary organizational change strategists such as Roger Martin and Dave Ulrich, have been captivated by the quest to understand and harness the essence of change. Yet the secret to mastering this elusive force is not rooted in rigid structural frameworks or narrowly defined objectives. Instead, it beckons us toward a more profound and nuanced comprehension of time and its pivotal role in the dynamics of change.

## Beyond the Horizon

Navigating the paradoxes of change is akin to sailing a ship through uncharted waters, relying on a combination of dead reckoning and celestial navigation. In this scenario, the captain must adeptly handle the unpredictable nature of the sea, using it as both a challenge and a guide. Dead reckoning, which involves constant adjustment based on the ship's known speed and direction, parallels the need for an ever-evolving approach in managing change; it's an ongoing, never static process. Similarly, celestial navigation requires understanding and interpreting the positions of stars and celestial bodies to chart a course, mirroring the need to look beyond the immediate and visible to guide decision-making in times of change. This concept often stands in stark contrast to traditional management theories that aim for control and predictability.

As we delve deeper into the nature of change, it's evident that ambiguity and uncertainty are not just inevitable but crucial components of transformation. This situation calls for adaptability and an enhanced sense of timing, vital for tackling both abrupt, event-driven changes like pandemics and technological disruptions, and the more gradual, evolutionary shifts. Change does not adhere to a linear path; it's replete with unexpected turns and twists, demanding a level of flexibility and resilience that is not prioritized by traditional management approaches.

Henry Mintzberg (1994), a well-known professor of management and organization, drew a key distinction between strategic planning and strategic thinking. Strategic *planning*, centered on predictability and control, often finds itself at odds with the fluid nature of change. Conversely, strategic *thinking*, much like the combination of dead reckoning and celestial navigation, involves embracing the unpredictability and ambiguity inherent in change. It champions adaptability, agility, and a readiness to accept unconventional solutions, advocating for a more dynamic, responsive approach that thrives amid the ever-changing challenges of change. Ultimately, strategic thinking requires leaders and organizations to develop a high tolerance for ambiguity, foster paradoxical thinking, and act with nimble agility in the perpetually evolving landscape of change.

# First Principles

In philosophy, science, and social science, there has been a notable shift in understanding organizations, both organic and human-made, influenced significantly by process philosophy and emergence theory. Moving away from focusing on static structures, these perspectives emphasize the dynamic, ever-changing nature of organizations. They advocate for viewing organizations not just in terms of their individual components but as a collective interplay of parts that adapt and evolve over time. This integrated approach underscores the importance of continuous adaptation and the interconnectedness within systems, reshaping our understanding of organizational dynamics. Process philosophy and emergence theory challenge reductionist views, focusing instead on the holistic, fluid nature of entities and the intricacies of change.

In mastering the paradoxes of change, a paradoxical mindset is not just beneficial—it's essential. This mindset is characterized by seven key principles: abundance of ideas, flexibility in thinking, risk-taking, curiosity, perseverance, openness to experience, and self-confidence. Together these principles form a dynamic foundation for individuals seeking to navigate the complexities and contradictions inherent in change. They enable us to generate multiple solutions, pivot strategies in the face of new information, embrace the unknown with courage, and maintain an insatiable desire for knowledge. Cultivating these principles fosters a deeply paradoxical mindset, equipping us well to master the paradoxes of change and thrive in an ever-evolving world.

At the opposite end of the spectrum on which the paradoxical mindset lies is what we call the either-or mindset, one that can only understand one position at a time. Let's explore the seven principles required for the paradoxical mindset and contrast them with the either-or mindset, demonstrating how these approaches impact real-life scenarios.

## Abundance of Ideas versus Single-Mindedness

**Paradoxical Thinking:** *Abundance of ideas.* In a world rife with para-doxes, your ability to generate a number of ideas becomes a cornerstone for paradoxical thinking. It doesn't matter that a lot of your ideas aren't even "good," because among those hundreds of ideas, some will be great. And as you continue to apply this principle, you will become more adept at generating larger quantities of good and great ideas.

An abundance of ideas enables you to envision multiple pathways through contradictions and challenges, making innovation a constant. To cultivate it, regularly engage your team in brainstorming sessions to explore various solutions to a problem, encouraging diverse perspectives and creative thinking. Collaborative and brainstorming sessions aren't just exercises in creativity; they are your training grounds for navigating the complexities of change, preparing you to swiftly adapt as situations evolve.

**Either-Or Thinking:** *Single-mindedness.* Adhering to a single-minded approach, you stick to one solution and resist exploring alternative ideas, which can limit innovation and adaptability. For example, you might focus solely on one strategy to solve a problem, dismissing other potential solutions without further consideration.

## Flexibility versus Rigidity

**Paradoxical Thinking:** *Flexibility in thinking.* When you are faced with the unpredictable nature of change and its inherent paradoxes, flexibility in thinking is indispensable. This principle allows you to pivot and adapt your strategies, embracing new information and unexpected shifts. Engaging with a variety of narratives and perspectives does more than broaden your cognitive flexibility; it equips you with the mental agility needed to reconcile conflicting ideas and navigate through the ambiguity of change. To cultivate this principle, remain open to changing your project plan when new information arises, ensuring the best possible outcome.

**Either-Or Thinking:** *Rigidity.* Sticking rigidly to a predetermined plan, you ignore new information and resist change, potentially leading to suboptimal results. You might refuse to adjust your project plan despite new evidence suggesting that a different approach would be more effective.

## Risk-Taking versus Caution

**Paradoxical Thinking:** *Risk-taking.* The essence of risk-taking in an ever-changing world lies in your willingness to confront the unknown and tackle the paradoxes head-on. By stepping out of your comfort zone and into uncertainty, you're not just innovating; you're actively choosing to adapt. The support of a community that encourages calculated risks illuminates the path through the complexities of change, fostering a culture of resilience and bold adaptation. For instance, you might propose and implement a novel strategy despite uncertainties, believing in its potential to drive significant improvement.

**Either-Or Thinking:** *Caution.* Preferring caution, you avoid taking risks and stick to familiar approaches, which can hinder innovation and growth. For example, you might choose not to pursue a promising but untested strategy, sticking to conventional methods instead.

## Curiosity versus Bias

**Paradoxical Thinking:** *Curiosity*. Curiosity propels you beyond the mere acquisition of knowledge; it drives you to question the status quo and explore the unknown, making it a vital principle for navigating the paradoxes of change. This incessant quest for understanding and the eagerness to learn from every situation enrich your adaptive capabilities, ensuring you remain open and responsive to the ever-evolving landscape of ideas and challenges. For example, you might actively seek feedback and new perspectives to continuously improve your understanding and approach.

 **Either-Or Thinking:** *Bias*. Relying on your bias, you stick to your current knowledge and beliefs, missing opportunities for growth and improvement. You might assume you know the best way to handle a situation, failing to seek input or consider new information.

## Perseverance versus Submission

**Paradoxical Thinking:** *Perseverance*. In the journey through the paradoxes of change, perseverance stands as your beacon of resilience. The relentless pursuit of your goals, despite the uncertainties and setbacks, underscores your capacity to adapt over time. Through your scientific explorations and personal endeavors, perseverance teaches you the importance of steadfastness in the face of adversity, reinforcing your adaptability in a world of constant flux. For instance, you might continue working on a challenging project despite setbacks, believing in the eventual success through persistent effort.

 **Either-Or Thinking:** *Submission*. Practicing submission, you may give up on challenging projects after a few setbacks, believing that change is not possible. You might abandon a project after encountering difficulties, accepting that it's too challenging to complete.

## Openness to Experience versus Familiarity

**Paradoxical Thinking:** *Openness to experience.* Openness to experience is your gateway to embracing the paradoxes of change. By welcoming new ideas, cultures, and experiences, you're both enriching your creative thinking and fostering an adaptive mindset that thrives on diversity and complexity. This openness is what enables you to navigate through contradictions and emerge with innovative solutions that address the multifaceted challenges of today's world. For example, you might enthusiastically participate in cross-cultural team projects, learning and integrating diverse perspectives.

**Either-Or Thinking:** *Familiarity.* Preferring familiarity, you stick to known methods and avoid new experiences, which can limit growth and innovation. You might only work with familiar team members and avoid cross-cultural collaborations, missing out on diverse insights.

## Self-Confidence versus Insecurity

**Paradoxical Thinking**: *Self-confidence.* Self-confidence is more than just a belief in your abilities; it's a critical component of your adaptive thinking arsenal. Self-confidence empowers you to face the paradoxes of change with a resilient and innovative mindset. It's this self-assurance that encourages you to venture into the unknown, experiment with new ideas, and embrace the complexity of change, thereby enhancing your capacity to adapt and thrive in an ever-evolving world. For instance, you might take on leadership roles in new projects, trusting in your ability to guide the team to success.

**Either-Or Thinking:** *Insecurity.* Mired in your insecurity, you might downplay your achievements and avoid taking on new challenges, which can limit your influence and growth. You might shy away from leading projects, doubting your ability to contribute effectively despite having relevant skills and experience.

By practicing these First Principles of paradoxical thinking, you embrace complexity and foster growth, both personally and professionally.

By contrast, either-or thinking, with its emphasis on single-mindedness, rigidity, caution, bias, submission, familiarity, and insecurity, can provide stability but often limits potential and hinders meaningful change. Embrace an abundance of ideas, flexibility in thinking, risk-taking, curiosity, perseverance, openness to experience, and self-confidence to navigate the paradoxes of change effectively and inspire others along the way.

# Change Theater

So many of the change programs that organizations run are what we call "change theater." They have catchy methodologies and use clever terms, but nothing really changes: the powerful remain powerful; the weak remain weak. The basic way in which the organization functions and preserves itself is the same over time. In fact, a lot of change programs are actually disguises to keep the organization the same. Leaders of organizations love to talk to their investors or their stakeholders about how much they're really changing, but they also want to stay leaders, and they see change as a threat to their power.

Most change initiatives fail to address the underlying paradoxes within the organization. As a result, they fail to make substantive changes. Paradoxical thinking is often used as a one-time event or a single practice during a crisis instead of an integral part of day-to-day operations, making leaders constantly lag behind the dynamics of change. Instead of continuously applying the paradoxical mindset, incorporating the needed change and adaptation in the organizational rhythm, and driving change, these leaders end up reacting to change. Thus, they are further perpetuating the cycle of change theater.

Change theater is characterized by grand gestures and surface-level adjustments that do not disrupt the core power structures and operational norms. These programs often serve to placate external stakeholders and create a façade of progress, while in reality, they maintain the existing state of affairs. Leaders boast about their transformational efforts to investors and stakeholders, but behind the scenes, they ensure that their positions and influence remain secure.

To break free from the cycle of change theater, leaders must undergo a radical shift in the way they think about change. Traditional approaches are insufficient because they don't challenge the status quo or address the deeper contradictions that hinder true transformation. Leaders need to move beyond superficial strategies and embrace a mindset that acknowledges and works through these paradoxes. This involves a continuous and integrated approach to paradoxical thinking, rather than a one-off exercise.

To truly innovate and drive meaningful change, leaders must view change as a continuous, evolving process rather than an episodic event. They must learn to navigate and leverage paradoxes as a central part of their strategy. By doing so, they can break free from the superficiality of change theater and initiate genuine transformation that reshapes their organizations from within. This approach requires courage, commitment, and a willingness to disrupt the status quo in pursuit of true organizational evolution.

## Understanding the Fundamental Nature of Paradoxes in Change

Change is inherently paradoxical. When you think about it, change involves contradictory yet interrelated elements. Growth and decline, for instance, are two sides of the same coin. Your organization cannot grow indefinitely without experiencing periods of decline and renewal. These contradictions don't just disappear; they coexist and need to be managed, not ignored or simplified. Ignoring these paradoxes causes many change efforts to fail.

Consider the dynamic cycle of change. It's never linear. You'll see phases of growth, decline, and renewal in any organization. Each phase brings unique paradoxes that must be addressed head-on. Recognizing and embracing this cycle is vital for successful change management. Remember, decline often leads to renewal, and the tension between these phases drives innovation.

Let's look at a personal example. In your career, you may experience a phase of rapid growth, gaining promotions and new responsibilities. This growth brings excitement and new challenges, but it also introduces extreme pressure and stress. You might feel exhilarated by new opportunities, yet simultaneously overwhelmed to the point of burnout. Eventually, you might hit a severe plateau or face a major setback, such as being abruptly demoted or even losing your job. This decline can shatter your confidence and lead to profound self-doubt. However, it also forces you into deep self-reflection and a reevaluation of your path. By confronting these intense challenges, acquiring new skills, or pivoting dramatically in your career, you can enter a powerful phase of renewal, discovering a renewed and profound sense of purpose and growth.

Now let's explore an organizational change example. Consider your organization's product development efforts. Launching a successful product can lead to rapid market expansion and increased revenue. However, this growth phase also brings challenges, such as maintaining quality and managing increased demand. Over time, market saturation or new competitors can cause a decline in sales. This decline forces your organization to innovate and adapt, perhaps by developing new products or improving existing ones, which in turn leads to renewed market interest and growth

## Embracing Leadership Challenges in Paradoxes

As a leader, you face the constant challenge of balancing competing values. Effective performance in your organization requires you to juggle these paradoxical demands. You need stability to ensure that current operations run smoothly, but you also need change to foster innovation and growth. It is in performing this balancing act that your leadership truly shines.

Your organization must exploit existing capabilities to maintain efficiency while also exploring new opportunities for growth. Striking this balance between exploitation and exploration is critical. It's what keeps your organization innovative and competitive in a rapidly changing environment. This duality is not easy to manage, but it's essential.

You also need to manage opposing yet interdependent elements within your organization. Think about promoting individual autonomy while maintaining collective coherence. These opposing forces can seem impossible to reconcile, but they are both necessary. Your role is to understand and foster an environment where such dualities can coexist and thrive.

## Navigating Effective Change Management

At the heart of effective change management lies a series of paradoxes that are not merely obstacles but essential drivers of transformation. The reason most change efforts fail is that they never fully address these underlying tensions. Instead of harnessing the generative power of these contradictions, organizations often attempt to compromise or balance them, leading to mediocre results. True innovation and growth occur when these paradoxes are embraced and used to create new and better ways for organizations—and individuals—to evolve. The structure and dynamics of organizations, much like those of individuals, require them to move through these paradoxes. Failing to do so risks reverting to previous, less effective ways of functioning.

Consider the story of Aaron and Olive, a married couple whose different upbringings create a significant tension in their marriage. Aaron grew up in a poor family, where money was always tight and the fear of accumulating debt was a constant presence. This background has made him deeply anxious about financial risk, and he is focused on paying down any debt as quickly as possible. For Aaron, security comes from knowing that they owe nothing to anyone and that their financial future is free from the burden of debt.

Olive, on the other hand, comes from a prosperous family that has always aggressively invested their money. Her parents taught her that taking calculated financial risks is the key to building wealth. Olive believes in using money to make more money, and she is eager to invest in opportunities that promise high returns, even if they come with some degree of risk. This approach has served her well in the past, and she is confident that continuing to invest aggressively is the best path to a secure and prosperous future.

These differing perspectives on money create a significant tension in their marriage. Aaron's focus on paying down debt clashes with Olive's desire to invest, leading to arguments and stress about how they should manage their finances. Each feels that the other's approach threatens their sense of security: Aaron fears that aggressive investments could lead to financial ruin, while Olive worries that an overly cautious approach will prevent them from achieving financial growth.

Instead of allowing this tension to erode their relationship, Aaron and Olive decide to explore a more imaginative solution that honors both of their perspectives. Instead of merely splitting their resources between debt repayment and investment, they conceive a creative financial strategy that blends their goals in a synergistic way.

They decide to establish what they call the "Revolving Wealth Fund." This fund operates like a revolving door between paying down debt and making strategic investments. The key feature of this fund is its fluidity— it allows money to move seamlessly between debt reduction and investment, depending on the couple's current financial needs and opportunities. Here's how it works:

Every time they make a payment toward reducing their debt, a portion of the interest saved is automatically redirected into the Revolving Wealth Fund. This money is then available to be invested in carefully chosen opportunities that offer the potential for growth without excessive risk. Conversely, when one of their investments yields a significant return, a portion of the profits is funneled back into the fund and earmarked for accelerating debt repayment.

But the revolving door concept goes further. To ensure that the couple maintains liquidity and can adapt to changing circumstances, the fund is designed to be highly flexible. If a promising investment opportunity arises, they can draw from the fund to seize it, knowing that the success of this investment will, in turn, contribute to faster debt elimination. On the other hand, if financial conditions tighten or their debt begins to feel burdensome, they can shift more of the fund's resources toward paying down the debt without compromising their investment strategy.

The Revolving Wealth Fund does more than just balance the couple's competing financial priorities—it actively enhances their financial strategy by turning their debt and investments into mutually reinforcing elements. This approach harnesses the constructive conflict in their marriage into a positive energy, resulting in a collaborative effort where both debt repayment and investment work together to build their financial future.

The imaginative nature of this solution also has a profound impact on Aaron and Olive themselves. Aaron begins to see that carefully managed investments can actually contribute to his goal of debt freedom, while Olive appreciates the security of knowing that their financial strategy is not just about growth but also about stability. These new perspectives help them grow both as individuals and as a couple, strengthening their relationship as they navigate the complexities of their financial lives.

Moreover, this experience teaches them valuable lessons that extend beyond their finances. They learn how to navigate the paradoxes in their relationship by finding solutions that honor both of their perspectives. This experience not only helps them achieve their financial goals but also deepens their mutual respect and understanding. They begin to apply this approach to other areas of their lives, finding that working through paradoxes together strengthens their marriage and helps them grow as individuals.

The story of Aaron and Olive illustrates how the tension between seemingly opposing goals can be a source of strength rather than conflict. By working through the paradox rather than avoiding it, they were able to create a solution that not only addressed their immediate challenges but also enhanced their relationship and set them on a path to shared success.

These paradoxes are at the core of change, and recognizing their role is crucial for any successful transformation. Organizations and individuals must engage with these tensions rather than avoid them. When managed correctly, paradoxes can become powerful tools that push the boundaries of what is possible. They challenge the status quo, forcing leaders—and individuals—to think creatively and strategically about how to move forward. This process of navigating and leveraging paradoxes ensures that change is not just a superficial adjustment but a deep, transformative shift that can sustain growth and adaptation over time.

Change efforts that fail to address these paradoxes are likely to revert to dominant, familiar patterns that are less effective in the long run. For instance, a couple that tries to balance opposing financial goals without truly integrating them may find themselves swinging between extremes—too cautious at times, too reckless at others. The key to overcoming this is to recognize that these tensions do not need to be balanced or compromised: they need to be used as a dynamic force for change. When individuals and couples learn to work through these paradoxes, they can create entirely new ways of functioning that are more resilient, innovative, and sustainable.

In essence, the success of any change initiative—whether in an organization or a relationship—hinges on understanding and navigating these paradoxes. They are not just peripheral issues; they are central to the process of transformation. By embracing and harnessing the power of these contradictions, you can drive meaningful, lasting change that not only addresses immediate challenges but also builds a foundation for future growth and success.

## Terra Incognita

When you're embarking on a new project at work, think of it as a voyage of discovery without a map. You have a general idea of what needs to be done, but the specifics are unclear. This is where the saying, "You don't know what you don't know until you know it" comes into play. It perfectly encapsulates the challenge of navigating through the unknowns. You might not realize what piece of information or strategy you're missing until you stumble upon it. This is the nature of dealing with complex, unfamiliar tasks—it's a process of exploration and understanding that evolves as you venture further into the work.

In the process of exploration, especially in a professional setting, you often encounter paradoxes that challenge conventional wisdom and defy logical expectations. This is particularly true when you're deeply experienced in your field. Ironically, extensive expertise can sometimes be a double-edged sword. It might lead you to believe you already have all the answers, inadvertently causing you to close your mind to new ideas or perspectives. In a world where situations and contexts are constantly evolving, clinging too tightly to what you think you know can blind you to innovative solutions or critical insights that could be pivotal for your project.

Therefore, when you are faced with new or challenging scenarios, it's crucial to remember that it's okay not to have all the answers right away. Embrace the opportunity to learn, adapt, and change your course as you gather more information. This approach to change is not merely about altering organizational strategies or processes; it's about fundamentally transforming how you think about problems and solutions. Being open to the possibility that there's always more to learn, and being flexible enough to integrate this new knowledge into your work strategy, are essential. This approach encourages you to evolve your thinking to stay relevant and effective in an endlessly changing landscape.

## The Paradoxes of Change

The following are the seven paradoxes we believe are among the most frequently encountered, and the most important, in managing change:

- We Seek to Change Others, but Can Only Change Ourselves
- We Aspire to Transcend Our Own Limits, but Must Do So from within Them
- We Use Facts to Change Minds, but Minds Aren't Changed by Facts
- We Set Goals for Change, but the Goals Change with the Change
- We Try to Minimize Conflict, but Change Is Created by It
- We Attempt to Avoid Failure, but All Learning Is Developmental and Requires Failure
- We Endeavor to Align the Change, but Change Is Driven by Deviance

Paradoxes, by their very nature, challenge our conventional thinking, presenting seemingly contradictory ideas that on deeper reflection offer profound insights. Change, too, is a complex phenomenon, often filled with contradictions that require both patience and urgency, stability and disruption. In this journey, these seven distinct paradoxes encapsulate the multifaceted challenges and opportunities of change. As we delve into each one, we'll uncover the intricate balance required to navigate the evolving landscapes of personal, organizational, and societal transformation.

All change ultimately begins with you: the individual. Self-understanding is the single greatest tool in a paradoxical mindset.

## Memory and Imagination

In the complexity of human cognition, memory and imagination are not just interconnected; they fundamentally shape our ability to adapt in a world of constant change. Memory doesn't simply archive our past; it actively interacts with imagination, blurring the lines between what was and what could be. This fusion empowers us to reinterpret our past experiences, using them as a foundation for innovative thinking and problem solving. The act of mentally revisiting past events becomes a strategic exercise, enabling us to extract lessons and apply them to future challenges. In this context, delving into our memories is a vital step toward constructing a more informed and imaginative future. Thus memory and imagination are critical tools in our cognitive arsenal, essential for navigating the unpredictable currents of change. This is why, throughout the book, we ask you to revisit your own past and identify standout, teachable moments in your life, which you will eventually bring together in a master personal narrative.

## Failure Is Instructive

In this book, we explore the nuanced relationship between failure and success, highlighting how each plays a crucial role in learning and growth. The stories you will read are drawn from our own experiences, a blend of both failures and successes. These are not extraordinary tales but rather relatable episodes from everyday life, reflecting the ups and downs we all face. Through sharing these stories, we aim to illustrate that failure is as instructive as success. As you read, we encourage you to reflect on your own moments of failure and success. Think about the lessons each experience taught you and how they've shaped your journey. The goal is to view each setback and victory as a critical step in your ongoing story, helping you navigate life with greater insight and resilience.

## Structure of This Book

In this book, you'll find each chapter focused on a different paradox of change. Each paradox is introduced through two stories, making it vivid and relatable. After each story, you'll find an explanation of paradox and its wider implications for your own everyday life. We then offer practical strategies and methods to help you work through these paradoxes ("Things to Try"). To deepen your engagement, there are four steps of the Paradoxical Mindset Cycle (described in the next chapter) to work through by thinking about your own experiences with change. We also encourage you to try small, manageable experiments or actions to start applying what you've learned by using the First Principles in analyzing your situations. This approach is focused on understanding change and finding ways to incorporate it in your own life.

## Point of View

In this book coauthored by Jeff and Staney, you'll delve into a series of true stories recounted from Jeff's perspective. These narratives offer more than just accounts—they provide you with Jeff's personal reflections and insights, giving you a genuine sense of what it's like to be an agent of change effecting real transformation. To ensure confidentiality, the names of individuals and organizations mentioned in the stories have been altered.

# CHAPTER 1

# The Paradoxical Mindset Cycle

**M**Y JOURNEY INTO THE WORLD of change and adaptation took me to an art museum in a quiet Midwestern town that had seen better days. I had decided to take on the commission because of my deep love for art. My client, the museum's director, Hamilton, was reporting to a board of civic-minded, influential stakeholders who held sway over the museum's fate.

The museum faced a daunting predicament. It possessed a substantial endowment, but the funds were strictly reserved for acquiring new artworks. Meanwhile, the aging institution cried out for repairs and updates: disability access, electrical upgrades, and the renovation of a dilapidated performance auditorium. Furthermore, the changing demographics of the city demanded a more inclusive collection that reflected underrepresented communities.

As I walked into the first meeting, I expected enthusiasm for Hamilton's vision of more inclusivity. To my surprise, not everyone on the leadership team was on board. The chief curator, Sebastian, insisted on adhering to a decade-old acquisition agenda approved by the board, fearing political backlash if they deviated. The head of the education department lamented their struggle to engage with local schools, as the existing artwork didn't directly resonate with the diversity of the community. The building manager pointed out that without essential repairs and updates, the museum's closure would render all other issues moot.

I observed these interactions, pondering the complexity of the situation. What was this resistance really about? Why was this happening now? What options did this team actually have? It was evident that for me to provide meaningful advice, I needed to invest more time than initially anticipated.

So I returned week after week for two months, delving deeper into the museum's ecosystem. Each visit involved interviews with key stakeholders, staff members, and museum visitors. I also explored the buildings and grounds comprehensively, seeking insights.

During one visit, Richard, the assistant curator, took me to a secured area where artwork was stored in a controlled environment. He unveiled a treasure trove of paintings by one of the most celebrated Flemish Baroque painters. My curiosity piqued, I asked why these masterpieces were not on display. Richard explained that there simply wasn't enough room to showcase them. He added a surprising tidbit: although the local community didn't flock to the museum, it was a mecca for art scholars worldwide who came to study these hidden gems tucked away in storage. In essence, these prestigious pieces were visible only to an elite few who had the credentials to study them.

With a little help, Richard formulated a daring proposal for the next leadership team meeting. To overcome the impasse, we proposed a bold experiment that had the potential to reshape the museum's future, for better or worse: What if we loaned the Flemish Baroque collection to a big museum on the East Coast? The fees generated could finance some of the crucial building renovations.

Sebastian vehemently opposed the idea, expressing concern about the fragility of the artwork and the exorbitant costs of repairing any damage. Richard, however, was undeterred. He conducted inquiries and found an interested East Coast museum willing to host the traveling exhibition. The condition was that the Midwest museum received full attribution for the collection and a fair share of the fees.

Over weeks of negotiations, we surmounted numerous obstacles, from joint-venture logistics to travel arrangements, insurance matters, and contractual agreements. Eventually, it was decided—the collection would embark on its journey.

The traveling exhibition exceeded our wildest expectations, drawing crowds and accolades. The museum not only profited from the show but also secured additional funding from foundations and the city itself, now basking in newfound prestige. Frustrated by the direction the museum was taking, Sebastian retired, and Hamilton followed suit months later. Richard, once the assistant curator, ascended to the positions of head curator and director.

The paradox lay in the necessity for Richard to stop thinking like a curator before he could start thinking adaptively like a leader. This transformation began with his aligning his mindset with the reality of the situation and then gradually influencing his colleagues to do the same.

# Change as Learning

As you delve into the nuances of the paradoxes of change, it becomes clear that at the core of navigating change and innovation is a process of relentless learning. This isn't just about gathering information; it's about discerning truths, testing what works, and being agile enough to shift perspectives as new insights surface. Through this continuous learning process, you'll develop your paradoxical mindset, which is a concept that Sara Beckman, a UC Berkeley business professor, and Michael Barry, a consultant and Stanford University engineer, eloquently explore in their article, "Innovation as a Learning Process: Embedding Design Thinking" (Beckman & Barry, 2007).

The paradoxical mindset is the cornerstone of change and innovation. Organizations that aim to be at the forefront of innovation need to foster environments that encourage this mindset, allowing for a fluid and flexible approach to new ideas and challenges. This adaptability is particularly crucial in our rapidly evolving technological landscape. The innovation process itself sets up a dynamic interplay between concrete experiences and abstract conceptualization, necessitating a blend of reflective observation and active experimentation. Here, the paradoxical mindset becomes indispensable, enabling you to navigate diverse modes of thinking and learning.

The paradoxical mindset becomes even more essential in developing a thriving team dynamics. In situations where the goals are somewhat ambiguous and complex, teams that encompass a variety of learning styles tend to outperform more homogenous groups. This diversity is a catalyst for innovation, as it brings together different perspectives and problem-solving approaches. However, it also increases the difficulties in managing conflicts effectively. In innovation, managing conflicts does not mean avoiding or resolving disagreements quickly to move on. Instead, it means transforming those differences into opportunities for growth and innovation. Moreover, it is crucial for team leaders to understand and accommodate the diverse learning styles of team members, producing an open and safe environment, robust discussions, and an inclusive process.

Furthermore, the importance of a paradoxical mindset extends to the observational research necessary for understanding user needs and context. In the innovation process, a deep and nuanced understanding of these elements comes through careful observation and analysis of complex information. A paradoxical mindset is vital here, allowing for a flexible and open approach to interpreting diverse data and insights.

## Thinking about Thinking

In the quest to stimulate profound and expansive thinking among students and adherents, educators and guides often employ intriguing elements such as the liar paradox: "Everyone is a liar." Statements like these are intentionally paradoxical and philosophical, aimed at prompting individuals to contemplate the inherent contradictions and complexities within them.

Rather than being unsolvable conundrums, these questions serve as deliberate paradoxes. They act as mirrors, encouraging individuals to turn their focus inward, to engage in a deeper exploration of their own cognitive processes. In essence, they are self-referential tools designed to disrupt the inertia of simplistic, habit-bound thinking. The goal is to encourage the development of a more mindful and adaptable perspective, one that entertains a wider range of responses and actions.

By delving into these kinds of paradoxes, teachers and guides aspire to nurture a heightened awareness of paradox as a concept. This awareness, in turn, inspires pupils and adherents to transcend the confines of conventional thought and embrace the intricate world of paradoxical ideas and actions. It is through the exploration of these enigmatic questions that individuals can embark on a journey toward greater intellectual depth and broader horizons of understanding.

## Tolerance of Ambiguity

As you navigate the complexities of change, certain traits stand out as beacons, guiding you toward success in both personal and professional realms. Drawing from the insights of E. Paul Torrance (1974, 1987) and E. O. Wilson (2017), pioneers in the field of creative thinking, we can identify these key traits. Their research not only highlights the characteristics of highly creative individuals but also offers a valuable framework for understanding how these traits intertwine with adaptability, providing guidance for personal and professional growth.

The implicit trait of both creative and paradoxical thinkers, a high tolerance of ambiguity, stands as a foundational pillar in these creative individuals' arsenal. This trait reflects their comfort with uncertainty and their ability to remain composed and decisive in situations where information is incomplete or outcomes are unpredictable.

Creative thinkers explore uncharted territories of imagination through their tolerance of ambiguity. When faced with unclear paths or undefined parameters, they do not shy away but rather embrace the opportunity to delve into the unknown. This tolerance allows them to navigate through creative processes with fluidity, unafraid of the ambiguous spaces where innovation often resides. In art, for example, artists frequently confront ambiguity as they seek to convey complex emotions or abstract concepts, using that ambiguity as a catalyst for creative expression and exploration.

Similarly, paradoxical thinkers leverage their high tolerance of ambiguity to navigate the complexities of change. In dynamic environments where circumstances are constantly shifting, they remain unfazed by uncertainty and ambiguity, embracing them as opportunities for growth and adaptation. Whether in business, where market conditions are unpredictable, or in personal life, where unexpected challenges arise, paradoxical thinkers approach ambiguity with resilience and adaptability, seeking solutions amid the flux.

The tolerance of ambiguity fosters a flexible and open-minded approach crucial for both creative and paradoxical thinkers. It enables them to explore diverse possibilities, entertain conflicting ideas, and make well-reasoned decisions even in the absence of complete information. Individuals with a high tolerance of ambiguity are less likely to experience stress in uncertain scenarios and are more open to a range of possibilities, making them adept at navigating through complex and ambiguous situations.

Ultimately, the tolerance of ambiguity serves as a catalyst for innovation and adaptation, enabling creative and paradoxical thinkers to thrive in environments characterized by rapid change and complexity. By embracing ambiguity, they unlock new avenues for exploration, discovery, and transformation, fueling their journey toward creative expression and adaptive success.

## Apply the Paradoxical Mindset Cycle

Drawing on established insights into creative thinking, the Paradoxical Mindset Cycle provides a structured approach for personal and professional development, rooted in the First Principles. This framework is crafted to empower you to effectively navigate and utilize paradoxes, transforming them into catalysts for growth and resilience. By engaging with the Paradoxical Mindset Cycle, you can leverage these paradoxes to achieve transformative breakthroughs across personal, interpersonal, and organizational dimensions.

### Step I: Find the Paradox

**Question to Answer:** Where do I notice contradictions, inconsistencies, or illogical parts in my story that don't seem to fit or make sense?

**Things to Do:** Identify moments where actions, decisions, or feelings clash with the rest of the narrative. Look for elements that feel out of place or confusing.

**How-To Tips**

A. *Tell the Story Multiple Times*

- Narrate your story several times, each time focusing on a different aspect.
- Change your perspective (e.g., from your point of view to another person's).
- Shift the tone (e.g., from emotional and subjective to logical and objective).
- Think of yourself as a writer who keeps to the facts but varies the storytelling approach.
- Take notes or record yourself to capture different versions.

B. *Look for the Paradoxes*

- Identify contradictions, incongruities, or parts that don't fit or make sense in your story.

**Example**

- Story: You love trees and live among many beautiful ones. During a snowstorm, a tree fell, blocking your road. You called a landscaper to remove them. Later, he suggested cutting down an apple blossom tree leaning toward your sunroom, and you agreed. You regretted it instantly, and were puzzled by why you made such an out-of-character decision.
- Paradox 1: Despite your love for trees and your creative problem-solving skills, you made an ill-advised decision to cut down the apple blossom tree. This contradiction is the paradox to explore.

## Step 2: Analyze the Meaning

**Question to Answer:** What underlying factors and insights can I uncover by examining from multiple perspectives and levels the paradox in my story?

**Things to Do:** Reflect on the facts and emotions to gain a deeper understanding of why the paradox exists and what it signifies.

**How-To Tips**

A. *Reflect on the Paradox*

- Seek to understand why there is a paradox and what it means.
- Consider what is really going on.
- Look for a story behind the story.
- Examine the cast of characters, the sequence of events, the setting, and so on.
- Draw insights from your reflections, identifying key themes, patterns, and insights.

B. *Interpret the Story on Multiple Levels*

- Objective level: Focus on the facts.
- Subjective level: Reflect on how you feel when you interpret the story in different ways.
- Symbolic level: Consider whether the story represents or points to something else.

**Example**

- Story: Upon reflection, you realize that you were in the middle of an emergency (the fallen tree blocking the road), and you were in a rapid, decisive, action-oriented mode. The landscaper introduced a new threat—the apple blossom tree might fall on your sunroom. At that time, you could not recognize that the situations of the two trees were different. While the fallen tree created an emergency situation, the apple blossom tree did not. You had alternatives to deal with the apple blossom: consulting your spouse, taking time to consider, or trimming the tree. But you did not consider any of them and acted impulsively. Delving deeper, you recognize that your desire to quickly remove the disruption led to a hasty, ill-advised decision.

- Paradox 2: Despite typically being thoughtful and creative, you made a rushed and ill-considered decision due to stress and urgency. This contradiction is the paradox to explore.

## Step 3: Establish Guiding Principles

**Question to Answer:** What key learnings from my story can be turned into guiding principles that will improve my effectiveness as a paradoxical thinker in future situations?

**Things to Do:** Reflect on the insights you've gained and identify specific aspects of the insights that can serve as actionable principles.

**How-To Tips**

A. *Capture Key Learnings*

- Reflect on the insights gained from analyzing the paradox.
- Identify specific aspects of these insights that can serve as guiding principles to enhance your paradoxical thinking.

B. *Create Guiding Principles*

- Incorporate new viewpoints that might lead to different outcomes.
- Consider how altering your behavior can create a more positive impact in future situations.

- Develop some guidelines or guardrails based on your key learnings so as to improve your paradoxical thinking (e.g., limits of actions, influence, effective communication strategies, timing).

- Think creatively about ways to remember these principles (e.g., visual aids, mnemonic devices, slogans, affirmations).

### Example

- Story: From the story of cutting down your apple blossom tree, you identified four obstacles to your paradoxical thinking: accepting advice too readily, making decisions too quickly, failing to consult your spouse, and wanting to resolve the situation effortlessly. On the basis of these obstacles, you create a simple guiding principle: When you're faced with an unexpected dilemma, give yourself permission and the appropriate amount of time to consider a wider range of possible options.

- Paradox 3: Despite valuing thorough decision-making and consultation, you bypassed these steps in a moment of urgency. This contradiction is the paradox to explore.

## Step 4: Implement Experiments

**Question to Answer:** What small, actionable changes can I implement based on my guiding principles so as to influence a broader context and improve my paradoxical thinking?

**Things to Do:** Identify specific, manageable experiments; implement them; and reflect on their outcomes to refine your approach.

**How-To Tips**

A. *Put Guiding Principles into Action*

- Identify a small, achievable change that can influence a broader context.

- Alter your response in recurring situations based on your guiding principles.

B. *Create and Implement a Plan*

- Develop a plan to achieve small wins.
- Diversify your approaches to discover what works and what doesn't.
- Ensure that your experiments are small in scale and carry limited risk while following your guiding principles.
- Try out the small change, then reflect on the results and make necessary adjustments.

**Example**

- Story: Imagine that your car unexpectedly stops working during a family vacation. A garage informs you of a severe problem, and you face a large, unexpected bill. Instead of rushing to make a decision, you choose to follow the guiding principle from the story of cutting down your apple blossom tree. You consult your spouse and explore options. You have the car towed to a nearby dealer, rent a car, and alter your vacation plan. The dealer repairs your car enough for you to drive home, saving you money and inconvenience. By applying your guiding principle, you practice paradoxical thinking and handle the situation more effectively.

- Paradox 4: Despite typically rushing to solve urgent issues, you took the time to explore options and consult other people, leading to a better outcome.

By considering creative and hybrid solutions and implementing them with intentionality, you can effectively navigate paradoxes and drive meaningful change. This approach encourages innovation, resilience, and sustained progress in both personal and organizational contexts. Step 4 is about taking action and observing the effects of your paradoxical mindset in real-world scenarios, promoting continuous learning and growth.

By methodically working through these steps and embracing the paradoxes encountered along the way, you develop a deeper paradoxical mindset, one that is crucial not only for personal growth but also for effective interpersonal and organizational relationships. Each step builds on the previous one, enhancing your ability to reflect on and intentionally navigate the complexities of change. This process helps you create significant breakthroughs by understanding and working within the often contradictory nature of change.

Look for opportunities to practice the First Principles—abundance of ideas, flexibility in thinking, risk-taking, curiosity, perseverance, openness to experience, and self-confidence—throughout your journey. These principles will serve as guiding lights, enhancing your adaptive capabilities and deepening your understanding of change's complexities. As you progress through the cycle, recognize that growth is a continual process, not a fixed endpoint. Explore your experiences, challenge assumptions, and adopt new perspectives.

## Knowing What We Know

In a world brimming with information and opinions, you need to navigate the seas of knowledge with a discerning eye. The most harmful people in our society are not necessarily those with malicious intentions but rather those who believe they possess certain knowledge when, in fact, they do not. This misconception becomes doubly dangerous when these individuals, often charismatic and persuasive, manage to convince others of their unfounded certainties.

Consider the sports commentators or stock market speculators who grace our television screens. Many of them simply reiterate what is already apparent to the discerning eye. However, when they venture out on a limb to make a bold prediction, their chances of being correct are often no better than those of a random guess. This reality is starkly evident when their advice, followed by many, leads to significant financial losses, including the erosion of hard-earned retirement savings. What motivates us to engage with their stories, heed their advice, or let their beliefs influence ours? Is it solely for amusement, a mirror of our self-doubt, or maybe a sign of our own indecisiveness? A paradoxical mindset may be our first and best defense against a world awash in noise.

# CHAPTER 2

# We Seek to Change Others, but Can Only Change Ourselves

Back in my college days, my journey through the complexities of personal and relational dynamics unfolded alongside Katie, a bright young woman whose vivacity was matched only by her steadfast chain-smoking habit. Our freshman-year romance blossomed amid the backdrop of my collegiate wrestling ambitions, offering a vivid tableau of contrasts and shared discoveries. Despite the myriad of qualities that drew me to her, Katie's smoking habit emerged as a silent battleground for my own evolving perspectives on change and influence.

Frustration simmered beneath my attempts to steer Katie toward a healthier lifestyle. Armed with facts and fueled by concern, I launched into a well-meaning yet naive crusade to alter her habits. I bombarded her with surgeon general reports and graphic depictions of smoking's toll, convinced that sheer logic would compel her to quit. But each fact I presented seemed to erect another barrier between us, widening the gulf of understanding.

In a desperate bid to shift her trajectory, I dangled the allure of a dream before her. I promised Katie an adventure in New York, the enchantment of Broadway awaiting her, should she agree to relinquish smoking. Yet my well-intentioned offer only served to highlight the chasm between our perspectives. The dream I painted faded against the reality of her addiction, leaving us both disheartened.

As the days passed, the weight of our struggle pressed on our relationship. Faced with the stubborn persistence of reality, I resorted to an ultimatum, starkly framing our bond against her smoking habit. The silence that followed my final gambit spoke volumes, marking the cessation of our connection and the beginning of a profound period of introspection for me.

Years later, in the unexpected serendipity of a grocery store encounter, the true nature of change revealed itself to me through Katie's transformation. Her once steadfast resolve to smoke had dissipated, replaced by a newfound determination to embrace a healthier lifestyle. But it wasn't coercion or bargaining that had sparked this change; it was her own volition, in her own time.

Her journey underscored the intricate dance of support, acceptance, and the gentle art of letting go. It taught me that the essence of influencing change lies not in imposing one's will but in offering a steadfast presence that empowers others to find their path.

This epiphany, gleaned from the echoes of a relationship defined as much by its challenges as by its moments of connection, illuminated the profound truth that change, both personal and collective, is a tapestry woven from the threads of patience, understanding, and the quiet strength of supportive companionship. It was a lesson in the subtlety of influence and the power of embodying the change one wishes to see, forever shaping my approach to navigating the nuanced landscape of human relationships and the ever-present paradoxes of change.

## Talking to Ourselves

In our journey toward mastering the paradoxes of change, experimental psychologist Ethan Kross's (2021) exploration in *Chatter: The Voice in Our Head, Why It Matters, and How to Harness It* serves as a critical guide to our internal dialogue and our emotion. Our internal dialogue often veers toward negativity, a formidable obstacle in embracing change and fostering a paradoxical mindset. Kross underscores the transformative power of reshaping this inner narrative. His ideas directly connect with the First Principles of abundance of ideas and flexibility in thinking. By cultivating an abundance of ideas, we learn to generate diverse solutions and perspectives, changing our inner voice from a source of self-criticism to a wellspring of creative thinking. Simultaneously, flexibility in thinking empowers us to pivot our thought processes amid the unpredictability of change, enabling us to view challenges as opportunities rather than as barriers. This adaptability is crucial especially when we are faced with difficult challenges, encouraging us to adopt mindful practices such as meditation, cognitive reframing, and self-compassion to foster a more positive and productive internal conversation. Kross's insights not only illuminate the path to mastering our inner chatter but also align perfectly with these foundational principles, guiding us to embrace change with creativity, resilience, and open-mindedness.

## THINGS TO TRY

To improve your ability to generate an abundance of ideas and flexibility in thinking by managing your internal "chatter," try these three simple exercises:

### Perspective Shift

Whenever you find yourself stuck in a loop of negative self-talk, pause and imagine what advice you would give to a friend in a similar situation. Write this advice down. This exercise helps create emotional distance, enabling you to view your circumstances more objectively and with greater compassion. By considering different perspectives, you can enhance your ability to generate an abundance of ideas.

### Future-Back Thinking

Take a moment to visualize how you will feel about your current challenge or situation one year from now. How significant will this issue be? What lessons might you have learned? This temporal distancing can help reduce the immediate stress and emotional impact the current challenge imposes on you, enabling you to think more clearly and flexibly about solutions and growth opportunities.

### Idea Journal

Keep a daily journal in which you write freely about any topic, concern, or idea that occupies your mind. Encourage yourself to explore these thoughts from various angles, without judgment. This practice not only helps in managing the chatter but also improves your ability to generate an abundance of ideas by encouraging a stream of consciousness that can lead to creative insights and solutions. Regularly reviewing your journal entries can also enhance your flexibility in thinking by revealing patterns and shifts in your thought processes over time.

---

These exercises aim to strengthen your mental agility, enabling you to navigate internal dialogues more effectively and adopt a more adaptive and creative mindset in the face of change.

## The Uncommon Good

When I was enlisted to help a law firm with its reinvention, I couldn't help but notice a figure who stood out amid the cacophony of conflicting opinions and self-interest. His name was Samuel, the eldest partner and a revered member of the leadership team. Samuel was a man of wisdom, an old hand who had seen it all in the legal world. Everyone liked him, and his counsel was often sought after, but at present, other than one person, Maya, few seemed willing to follow Samuel's advice.

Samuel had been the one who had brought me in as a consultant, recognizing that an external perspective might navigate the firm through some tumultuous times. He saw something in Maya that others might have missed. Perhaps it was his own experience that made him appreciate Maya's approach, one that was rooted in the wisdom of the ages.

As the discussions continued and the tensions within the leadership team escalated, Samuel quietly observed from the sidelines. He rarely spoke up during the meetings, allowing the voices of the more assertive partners to dominate the conversation. But when he did speak, his words carried the weight of years of experience.

One day, during a particularly heated debate, Samuel finally decided to address the room. His voice was calm, his words measured: "We find ourselves at a crossroads, torn between the immediate gains and the long-term health of our firm. I've seen firms rise and fall, and I can tell you this—the path to true success lies in aligning our interests with the common good of this firm."

His words hung in the air, and for a moment, the room fell silent. Samuel's gaze then shifted toward Maya, who was listening intently. "Maya here," Samuel continued, "has shown us a path that combines personal sacrifice with strategic thinking. She's willing to invest in the future of our firm, not just for herself but for all of us."

The room was divided. Some partners were skeptical; others were intrigued by Samuel's perspective. But it was Maya who broke the silence. "I believe in what Samuel is saying," she declared. "I've seen the positive impact of investing in our team, and I'm willing to take it a step further. I'll cut a significant portion of my payout to support this vision."

It was a pivotal moment. Maya's willingness to make a personal sacrifice for the greater good resonated with some partners, and a new direction began to take shape. Slowly but surely, the firm started to shift its focus toward building a sustainable future, just as Samuel had suggested.

Maya's approach became the catalyst for change within the firm. Her mergers-and-acquisitions team flourished, attracting top talent and winning high-profile deals. And as the firm's fortunes improved, so did

Maya's own career prospects. She was offered an executive-team position at a large global private equity firm, a testament to the power of her long-term thinking and commitment to the firm's greater good.

Reflecting on this journey, I realized that our own actions have the power to transform the organizations we are a part of. Samuel's wisdom, Maya's self-sacrifice, and the firm's willingness to embrace a new vision had reshaped its destiny. In the end, it was not just about attracting and retaining talent or maintaining partner income; it was about building a legacy that would benefit all. And this journey began with a leader who was willing to change herself for the common good of the firm.

# Reflections of the Self

In his article "Moments of Greatness: Entering the Fundamental State of Leadership," organizational change and culture expert Robert E. Quinn (2005) articulates a transformative approach to leadership, advocating for a shift from seeking comfort to engaging in results-centered action. Quinn's paradigm challenges leaders to embrace risk and flexibility, two fundamental principles essential for navigating the complexities of change. By advocating for setting clear, ambitious goals, Quinn underscores the importance of risk-taking in driving innovation and growth. Simultaneously, he emphasizes the necessity of flexibility in thinking, encouraging leaders to remain adaptable and open to new perspectives, which is crucial for steering through uncertainties.

At the core of Quinn's philosophy is the alignment of personal actions with deeply held values, which ensures that decisions reflect authenticity and integrity. This alignment is pivotal in fostering genuine leadership, characterized by a commitment to collective goals and mutual growth. Quinn also highlights the significance of embracing feedback and new ideas, positioning them as opportunities for improvement and innovation. This openness to diverse viewpoints keeps leaders relevant and adaptable, enabling them to thrive in fast-evolving environments.

Embarking on this leadership journey entails stepping out of one's comfort zone to actively shape outcomes. This process begins with setting specific goals that improve team dynamics, achieve personal milestones, or launch new initiatives. Breaking down these goals into manageable tasks enables leaders to transition from responding passively to engaging proactively. A deep dive into personal values such as integrity, innovation, and teamwork further guides decision-making, ensuring that actions are a true reflection of the leader's core beliefs.

In the professional realm, leaders can amplify impact by aligning their individual ambitions with organizational objectives. This alignment might involve their sidelining personal projects to address pressing team needs, fostering a culture of collaboration. Moreover, a leader's actively seeking feedback from peers and being open to challenging ideas are essential practices. They not only invite constructive criticism but also stimulate a culture of continuous learning and adaptability.

In essence, Quinn's exploration offers a blueprint for leadership that transcends conventional practices. By adopting a results-centered approach, grounded in risk-taking and flexibility, leaders can transform their environments. This dynamic interplay of setting clear goals, aligning with personal values, and fostering an environment of feedback and collaboration empowers leaders to navigate change effectively, embodying the principles of positive transformation.

## THINGS TO TRY

Improving risk-taking and flexibility in thinking involves stepping out of your comfort zone and being open to new perspectives. Here are simple exercises to cultivate these qualities:

### Goal-Setting with a Twist

Identify a professional goal, then challenge yourself to achieve it through a method outside your usual approach—

41

for example, by delegating more, seeking cross-departmental collaboration, or incorporating feedback from a wider array of colleagues. Reflect on how this different approach affects the outcome and your ability to adapt.

### Values Audit

List your top five personal values and look at them in the context of recent decisions you've made at work. Where do they align, and where do they diverge? Use this insight to adjust future decisions, ensuring that they more closely reflect your core values, enhancing your authenticity and flexibility in problem solving.

### Feedback Loop

Create a monthly feedback session with peers from different departments or expertise areas in your organization. Openly share challenges and seek your peers' perspectives, focusing on understanding viewpoints vastly different from your own. This practice not only broadens your thinking but also prepares you to adapt more fluidly to changes and challenges.

## One Size Never Fits All

Our limited ability to change others despite our boundless capacity to influence them underscores the importance of recognizing everyone's unique journey. Each person is propelled by a mix of motivators, from seeking personal growth to aspiring for professional achievements or spiritual fulfillment. Embracing the principles of abundance of ideas, flexibility in thinking, and risk-taking can guide us in this endeavor. These concepts encourage us to explore a variety of solutions, remain adaptable in our thinking, and embrace the uncertainties inherent in taking risks.

Applying these principles helps us approach interactions with empathy, appreciating the diverse motivations that drive individuals. This approach not only enhances our ability to positively influence those around us but also empowers us to navigate our own challenges with resilience and creativity. As we move forward, let's carry these insights with us, fostering environments that encourage growth, adaptability, and the courage to face change with confidence.

# Apply the Paradoxical Mindset Cycle: We Seek to Change Others, but Can Only Change Ourselves

Reflect on your past experiences where you attempted to change some—one else's behavior, attitude, or beliefs.

## Step 1: Find the Paradox

**Question to Answer:** Where do I notice contradictions, inconsistencies, or illogical parts in my attempts to change others while neglecting my own need for change?

**Things to Do:** Identify moments where actions, decisions, or feelings clash with the rest of the narrative. Look for elements that feel out of place or confusing.

## Step 2: Analyze the Meaning

**Question to Answer:** What underlying factors and insights can I uncover by examining the paradox of focusing on changing others instead of addressing my own internal challenges?

**Things to Do:** Reflect on the facts and emotions to gain a deeper understanding of why the paradox exists and what it signifies.

## Step 3: Establish Guiding Principles

**Question to Answer:** What key learnings can I turn into guidelines that help me to address my own internal challenges instead of focusing on changing others?

**Things to Do:** Reflect on the insights you've gained and identify specific aspects of those insights that can serve as actionable principles.

## Step 4: Implement Experiments

**Question to Answer:** What small, actionable changes can I implement based on my guiding principles to shift my focus from changing others to fostering my own personal growth?

**Things to Do:** Identify specific, manageable experiments; implement them; and reflect on their outcomes to refine your approach.

## PRACTICE THE FIRST PRINCIPLES: WE SEEK TO CHANGE OTHERS, BUT CAN ONLY CHANGE OURSELVES

### Abundance of Ideas

Use your creativity to find various ways to change your own behaviors and attitudes, understanding that by improving yourself, you create a ripple effect that can inspire others to change.

### Flexibility in Thinking

Adapt your thinking to accept that although you cannot directly change others, you can change how you interact with and respond to them, which may influence their behavior over time.

## Risk-Taking

Take the risk of focusing on self-improvement instead of trying to change others, recognizing that this shift in focus may initially feel uncomfortable but can lead to more meaningful and sustainable change.

## Curiosity

Cultivate curiosity about your own patterns and motivations, exploring how your actions and attitudes impact your relationships and how changing yourself can lead to new and positive dynamics.

## Perseverance

Persist in your efforts to change yourself, even when doing so feels challenging or when you are tempted to revert to trying to change others, knowing that personal growth is a continuous journey.

## Openness to Experience

Be open to the experiences and insights that come from focusing on your own change, embracing the opportunities for learning and growth that arise from this introspective approach.

## Self-Confidence

Build your self-confidence by acknowledging and celebrating your progress in changing yourself, understanding that this self-assuredness can serve as a powerful example and will influence others indirectly.

## CHAPTER 3

# We Aspire to Transcend Our Own Limits, but Must Do So from within Them

A SPEAKING ENGAGEMENT AT A NOTABLE medical conference set the stage for a transformative experience of my own. I never anticipated that an executive representing a major medical center in New York City would approach me afterward to enlist my assistance in leading a substantial change initiative.

The ensuing project was to significantly reduce the amount of time it took for cardiovascular surgery patients to recover effectively and be discharged back to their respective cardiologists. At issue was more than just the application of advanced surgical methods or the use of new technology to more accurately assess the condition of patients. Many of the challenges stemmed from an apparently toxic culture in the medical center, exacerbated by the hierarchy of the organizational structure.

A venerable member of the medical center's advisory board asked me to partner on the project with a brilliant young physician-turned-consultant at the most prestigious management consulting company in New York. I cautiously agreed. My collaboration with Aarav, a highly educated doctor, became a dynamic partnership. His deep medical knowledge complemented my expertise in organizational change.

As we delved into the project, our first challenge became gaining the trust of the medical staff, who understandably questioned my limited understanding of their complex world. This contrast between my superficial grasp of medicine and Aarav's virtuosity eventually became an asset; we learned to collaborate effectively.

One pivotal moment occurred during an off-site retreat with the hospital's esteemed doctors, where we encountered the formidable Dr. Rick, a renowned cardiovascular surgeon and respected leader. Dr. Rick openly questioned my qualifications, portraying me as an academic with theories but no practical experience. Tensions ran high until I shared a bit of my background, discussing my experience in building a successful company from scratch and my modest education from a state school—details that surprisingly resonated with Dr. Rick's own beginnings. This common ground bridged the gap between us.

With Dr. Rick and Aarav now as allies, we embarked on a transformational journey, replete with its fair share of challenges. We took key members of the leadership team on field trips to top medical centers to benchmark best practices. Teams were formed to reengineer key processes, paying particular attention to those that stretched between units such as radiology and anesthesiology. Administrative units were restructured, and biweekly town hall meetings were put in place to gain constant feedback and make real-time adjustments to the operation of the medical center.

We continually measured our progress against that of other leading medical centers, gradually witnessing the fruits of our labor. The ultimate reward was an unforeseen merger with another prestigious medical institution, resulting in one of the largest health care conglomerates of its kind at that time.

This experience underscored a valuable life lesson. My initial lack of medical knowledge proved to be not a hindrance but a unique opportunity for collaboration and learning. Because I recognized my limitations and leveraged the strengths of others, such as Aarav and Dr. Rick, together we successfully propelled substantial change.

My immersion into the realm of medicine was an intensive crash course of rapid learning. After my initial involvement with the medical center's change initiative, I quickly realized that my success was contingent on grasping the intricacies of the health care world.

My learning journey began with long hours spent watching surgeries with unwavering focus. I gained insights into the necessary precision and skill the surgeons need to bring into these medical procedures with high stakes. My thirst for knowledge extended beyond the operating room; I spent days shadowing various hospital units, ranging from radiology to cardiology and beyond. This hands-on exposure provided me with a profound understanding of the daily challenges, workflows, and demands of each department.

Simultaneously, while I immersed myself in medicine, the doctors, nurses, and medical staff were undergoing their own learning process—adapting to change. We learned from one another, and the process of change was undeniably messy; learning came through action and experience rather than traditional classroom-style instruction.

The medical staff had to embrace new workflows, technologies, and ways of operating. This transition proved challenging, and resistance surfaced at times. However, as we adapted, iterated, and refined our approach, we all gained confidence. People made mistakes, but they served as stepping stones toward improvement. The appropriate competencies and a culture that accepted change developed slowly, and only through experience.

Then came the unexpected twist—the merger with another leading medical institution. This development added even more complexity to our learning journey, compelling us to reassess and relearn many aspects of our change initiative. Integrating medical practices, merging organizational cultures, and navigating the politics of change presented significant challenges. However, the changes we had already implemented in our own medical center equipped us to handle these complexities more effectively. Our team was much better prepared to deal with the integration, having developed the competencies and culture that embraced change. In the end, the merger stood as a testament to our collective adaptability and resilience in the face of complexity. It underscored the principle that learning is an ongoing journey, often driven by embracing the unexpected and the unknown.

## Know What You Don't Know

The concept of a "beginner's mindset" is a stark contrast to the commonly heard phrase "Fake it till you make it." Although the latter may have its place in certain contexts, it carries a misguided implication when applied to professions that demand expertise, precision, and accountability, such as surgery or aircraft maintenance.

In these critical fields, the phrase "Fake it till you make it" can devalue the importance of genuine expertise and the responsibilities that come with it. A surgeon cannot simply pretend to be a skilled practitioner, nor can an aircraft maintenance mechanic bluff their way through complex machinery. Instead, the path to mastery begins with acknowledging what one does not know and embracing the imperative to learn through practical experience, all under the watchful support and guidance of those who have genuinely mastered their craft.

A true beginner's mindset fosters an environment where individuals approach their tasks with an open heart and mind, much like novices eager to explore the unknown. It emphasizes the willingness to learn, adapt, and remain receptive to possibilities, regardless of one's current level of expertise or familiarity with the subject matter.

In her article "Beginner's Mind: Paths to Wisdom That Is Not Learned," psychologist Eleanor Rosch (2008) delves into the concept of the beginner's mind and its significance in cultivating a state of openness and creativity. Rosch explores this through various spiritual traditions, highlighting the importance of adopting a beginner's mindset in adult life to foster inner wisdom and a more fulfilling existence.

Embarking on a journey toward adopting a beginner's mindset can transform how you engage with the world, fostering a deeper connection to life's inherent wisdom and creativity. Adopting a beginner's mindset, grounded in the principles of curiosity and openness to experience, fundamentally shifts how we approach learning and problem solving.

This approach is especially relevant in fields where precision is crucial, underscoring the importance of genuine expertise. Unlike the "Fake it till you make it" mindset, which suggests a superficial acquisition of knowledge, a beginner's mindset encourages a thorough and humble exploration of what we do not know. It compels us to ask questions, seek new experiences, and remain open to revising our understandings based on new information. This continuous loop of learning, unlearning, and relearning is not just about accumulating knowledge but about enhancing our ability to engage with complex issues creatively and effectively. It transforms every new challenge into an opportunity for growth, ensuring that we are always evolving, both professionally and personally.

## THINGS TO TRY

Here are three key practices you can apply to cultivate a beginner's mind:

### Embrace Curiosity in Every Moment

To truly embrace curiosity, approach every situation with a sense of wonder, as if seeing it for the first time. This means asking "why" and "how" questions that a child might ask, fostering a genuine interest in understanding the world around you. Allow yourself to dive into new hobbies or subjects that spark your interest, regardless of their immediate relevance to your current skills or knowledge. Such exploration is not about achieving proficiency in the future but about the joy of learning itself in the present. Furthermore, dedicate time each day to reflect on something new you've discovered or a perspective you hadn't previously considered. This reflective practice can deepen your appreciation for the vastness of knowledge and experience available to you, fueling your curiosity even further.

## Cultivate Openness to Diverse Experiences

Actively seek out new and unfamiliar experiences as a way to step out of your comfort zone. This could involve traveling to new places, trying out different cuisines, or engaging in conversations with people whose life experiences vastly differ from your own. When you are faced with ambiguity or uncertainty, try to embrace it rather than seeking immediate resolutions. This openness to uncertainty can be a rich source of personal growth and insight. To further enhance this aspect, engage in mindfulness practices to remain present and nonjudgmental about each moment. Mindfulness enables you to experience the full depth of the present, enriching your life with a broader spectrum of experiences and deepening your empathy and understanding of others.

## Unlearn to Learn

Journaling can be a powerful tool for identifying and challenging deeply held beliefs or assumptions. By writing about your experiences from a fresh perspective, you can begin to see them in a new light, questioning what you thought you knew. Engage in dialogues with the intention of understanding rather than convincing, listening rather than speaking. This open exchange of ideas can be incredibly fruitful, enabling you to adjust your views based on new insights. Adopt a stance of "not-knowing," which acknowledges that there is always more to discover. Approaching problems and learning opportunities with humility and openness to new solutions can lead to innovative thinking and deep, meaningful learning. This process of unlearning in order to make room for new knowledge and insights is challenging but crucial for maintaining a beginner's mind. It is this continuous cycle of curiosity and openness that allows for lifelong growth and discovery.

# Show and Tell

Thanks to my extensive experience in transforming and innovating organizations, I received an invitation to speak at a conference attended by business school deans. The topic of my address was focused on the theme "The Business School of the Future: What It Is and How to Create It." The deans were already familiar with my successful track record in navigating intricate change initiatives, and I felt deeply honored to have the opportunity to engage with them.

In my speech, titled "The Future Has Come and Gone and You've Missed It" (DeGraff, 2015), I positioned myself as an agent of radical change. I passionately criticized the audience's conservative approaches, highlighting their reluctance to embrace the evolving landscape of business education. I fervently advocated for a fresh wave of creativity, innovation, and adaptability, believing that my words alone would be enough to inspire the transformation they needed. I was a seasoned changemaker, and I believed that my knowledge and insights would be sufficient to lead them toward the path of progress.

Many of these deans were brilliant academics in various fields of study, yet lacked real-world business experience. By contrast, having built several large businesses and organizations, I possessed valuable practical insight. However, since I didn't effectively communicate this hands-on tradecraft and real-world experience, my words failed to reach the audience. The deans and I missed an opportunity to collaborate meaningfully in making substantive change in business education.

In my zeal to challenge these deans' entrenched practices, I failed to grasp a fundamental aspect of my role: the obligation to lead by example. I had the opportunity to start a meaningful conversation with them, collaborate with them sincerely, to roll up my sleeves and actively guide them through the process of change. I possessed the knowledge and experience to demonstrate how to implement the changes I was so ardently promoting. Yet I opted for rhetoric over action, delivering a message of revolution without the commitment to facilitate it.

This was a glaring oversight and a reflection of my own hypocrisy. While I was quick to point out their resistance to change, I was not taking the necessary steps to help them overcome it. Rather than moving beyond words and into tangible actions, I'd held back, choosing the safety of my established position over the risks and challenges of genuine changemaking.

The epiphany hit me hard. I could have used my knowledge and experience to lead these deans into a new era of educational innovation. Instead, I remained on the sidelines, a critic rather than a collaborator. This experience served as a valuable lesson, teaching me that effecting change requires more than just challenging the status quo; it demands active involvement and a willingness to be part of the solution.

## Apprenticing the Sorcerer

To transcend our limits, we always have to start by acknowledging them: the limits of our knowledge, the limits of our resources, the limits of our time. Once we acknowledge those limits, it's time to facilitate lots of experiences and as many experiments as possible to continually grow.

There are two fundamentally different ways of doing this. The first is to develop and expand our skills under the tutelage of people with more advanced skills or, if you're an autodidact, through (very) disciplined self-development. The second is by running experiments, trying out many different things at once and seeing what works. These two approaches are not mutually exclusive. You can certainly seek out mentors while also carrying out many experiments.

In their book *Deep Smarts: How to Cultivate and Transfer Enduring Business Wisdom*, Harvard business professor Dorothy Leonard and Tufts psychology professor Walter Swap (2005) offer useful strategies for developing new talents and skills to help us move beyond our current abilities. The authors emphasize the inadequacy of traditional methods of knowledge transfer, such as documentation and lectures, in conveying the tacit know-how that forms the essence of deep smarts. This tacit knowledge, often developed through years of experience, is hard to document and cannot be easily transferred through conventional means.

Actual learning occurs only through doing. *Deep Smarts* suggests a shift toward more interactive and experiential learning techniques. The authors highlight guided problem solving, observation, practice, and Socratic questioning as effective methods for fostering active learning. These approaches encourage learners to engage directly with real-world scenarios, enabling them to build and apply their knowledge in specific contexts. Such methods are in contrast to passive forms of learning, such as lectures or presentations, which are less effective in transferring deep, context-specific knowledge.

When contemplating your own journey of growth and development, it's essential to recognize a continuum: on one end lies passive reception, where we absorb information from mentors, books, or lectures, and on the other end lies active learning, where we engage in hands-on experimentation and problem solving. Finding the balance between seeking guidance from those with more experience and actively testing and iterating our own ideas is key. By combining the insights gained from mentors or resources like *Deep Smarts* with hands-on experimentation, we can cultivate both breadth and depth of knowledge, ultimately driving meaningful change and growth in our endeavors.

## THINGS TO TRY

To maximize learning effectiveness, try these exercises:

### Engage in Interactive Learning Techniques

Prioritize interactive and experiential methods such as guided problem solving, observation, and practice. These hands-on approaches enable you to directly engage with real-world scenarios, facilitating the application and consolidation of knowledge in specific contexts.

### Seek Mentorship and Real-World Experience

Establish regular meetings with mentors to discuss industry trends and insights, drawing from their experiences to enhance your understanding. In addition, volunteer for projects that provide opportunities for you to apply new skills in practical settings so that you gain firsthand experience and reinforce your learning.

### Foster a Culture of Continuous Learning

Encourage innovation and learning within your team by organizing brainstorming sessions to tackle challenges creatively. Emphasize the importance of breaking down complex problems into manageable tasks, promoting experiential learning and adaptation for both personal and professional growth.

# See One, Do One, Teach One

The journey to mastery starts with apprenticeship, whereby you glean wisdom under the expert tutelage of seasoned mentors and hone your skills. As you advance, your voyage moves into a realm of experimentation, where you put acquired knowledge to the test. This is the crucible where you dare to challenge boundaries and embrace the lessons of your mistakes. Your mentor becomes your compass, offering wisdom and perspective to navigate the numerous challenges in your voyage of discovery. Ultimately, mastery unfolds as a synthesis of the knowledge bestowed by mentors and the wisdom amassed through your own trials and experiments. The continuous synthesis of more passive and active learning perpetually propels you toward higher echelons of proficiency and insight.

In the voyage of personal and professional growth, you stand at the crossroads where aspiration meets limitation. This existential paradox of change encompasses your recognition of the inherent constraints stemming from your physical form, cultural background, and economic circumstances. So how do you navigate this enigmatic paradox? The key lies in distinguishing between lofty, unrealistic dreams and pragmatic, attainable plans for transformation. Authentic growth necessitates acknowledging and operating within your limitations, not in defiance of them.

## THINGS TO TRY

One powerful approach to transcending your limits is the See One, Do One, Teach One method, a principle deeply rooted in practical learning and skill acquisition, used extensively in training doctors and skilled tradespeople.

### See One

The journey begins with observation. Like a medical student watching an experienced surgeon, you start by learning from those who have mastered the skills you aspire to acquire. This stage is about immersion and understanding; you absorb knowledge and gain insights into the complexities of the task at hand.

### Do One

Next, you transition from observer to practitioner. This is where your learning takes shape in the real world. You apply what you've seen, experimenting and adapting it to your own context. It's a stage filled with trials and errors, each mistake a lesson in itself. Here, within the safety of your known limits, you begin to push the boundaries, extending your capabilities bit by bit.

### Teach One

Finally, the cycle of learning comes full circle when you teach others. Teaching is not just an act of imparting knowledge; it's a process that deepens your own understanding and mastery. As you articulate what you've learned and guide others, you solidify your own skills and often gain new insights. You evolve to become a guide for others.

In this journey, the value of practicality is paramount, echoing the philosophy of John Dewey (1910, 1916), an American advocate of pragmatism. Dewey's belief was that learning thrives as an active, hands-on process, encompassing observation, engagement, and teaching. This pragmatic approach highlights each phase as a crucial step in broadening your skills and extending the reach of your knowledge.

In embracing this See One, Do One, Teach One approach, you acknowledge the paradoxes of change. You understand that transcending your limits does not mean discarding your current self but expanding from within the framework of your existing capabilities. It's a journey of mindful growth, with lots of courage, where each step forward is both a recognition of where you are and an aspiration of where you wish to be.

## Apply the Paradoxical Mindset Cycle: We Aspire to Transcend Our Own Limits, but Must Do So from within Them

Reflect on past experiences when you were learning something completely new.

## Step I: Find the Paradox

**Question to Answer:** Where do I notice contradictions, inconsistencies, or illogical parts in my efforts to transcend my limits while needing to acknowledge and work within them?

**Things to Do:** Identify moments where actions, decisions, or feelings clash with the rest of the narrative. Look for elements that feel out of place or confusing.

## Step 2: Analyze the Meaning

**Question to Answer:** What underlying factors and insights can I uncover by examining the paradox of striving for growth and transcendence while operating within my current limitations?

**Things to Do:** Reflect on the facts and emotions to gain a deeper understanding of why the paradox exists and what it signifies.

## Step 3: Establish Guiding Principles

**Question to Answer:** What key learnings from my attempts to transcend my limits can be turned into guiding principles that will help me balance aspiration with acceptance of my current reality?

**Things to Do:** Reflect on the insights you've gained and identify specific aspects of those insights that can serve as actionable principles.

## Step 4: Implement Experiments

**Question to Answer:** What small, actionable changes can I implement based on my guiding principles to better navigate and gradually expand my limits?

**Things to Do:** Identify specific, manageable experiments; implement them; and reflect on their outcomes to refine your approach.

## PRACTICE THE FIRST PRINCIPLES: WE ASPIRE TO TRANSCEND OUR OWN LIMITS, BUT MUST DO SO FROM WITHIN THEM

### Abundance of Ideas

Brainstorm a variety of approaches for self-improvement and professional growth that leverage your existing strengths and resources for you to grow.

### Flexibility in Thinking

Embrace the need to adapt your strategies and thinking patterns to navigate the constraints of your current situation, finding creative ways to make progress even when facing obstacles.

### Risk-Taking

Challenge yourself to take calculated risks within your current limitations, such as proposing a new project at work or learning a new skill, understanding that pushing boundaries can lead to significant personal growth.

### Curiosity

Cultivate curiosity about your own habits and routines, questioning how they might be holding you back and exploring new methods and perspectives that can help you overcome these self-imposed limits.

## Perseverance

Maintain a persistent effort to achieve your goals, even when progress is slow or setbacks occur, recognizing that steady, determined action is key to gradually pushing beyond your limits.

## Openness to Experience

Actively seek out and embrace new experiences that can provide fresh insights and skills, using these experiences to expand your capabilities from within your current context.

## Self-Confidence

Build your self-confidence by reflecting on and celebrating your successes and progress, no matter how small, reinforcing your belief in your ability to achieve your aspirations despite any limitations you currently face.

## CHAPTER 4

# We Use Facts to Change Minds, but Minds Aren't Changed by Facts

DURING A CHANCE ENCOUNTER I had in my hometown of Kalamazoo, Michigan, an old acquaintance named Sue, who had connections to my parents, brought up an intriguing local initiative known as the Kalamazoo Promise. This program, unlike any other in the US, guaranteed tuition for higher education to every high school graduate in Kalamazoo, aiming to bridge the gap between lower-income and middle-class students. As we talked about it, I felt a personal connection. Sue, surprised but pleased to hear that I had earned my doctorate, noted that the Kalamazoo Promise was designed to help students like the one I had been.

Sue enthusiastically described the program's promotional strategies, efforts to engage parents, and streamlined processes designed to make higher education attainable for Kalamazoo's youth. Despite her unwavering optimism, I couldn't help but express some reservations. I pointed out potential obstacles, such as financial constraints, family commitments, lack of preparation, and physical and mental health.

Although the Kalamazoo Promise made national headlines and served as a model for other cities striving to bridge the education gap, its success was not universal. The Kalamazoo Promise was indeed a lifeline to a brighter future for some students, but its benefits remain elusive to others. Despite the program's initial acclaim, the reality on the ground revealed a more nuanced picture of its impact, showcasing the complexities inherent in addressing systemic inequalities.

A decade later, an article brought back memories of that conversation, revealing an unexpected twist of fate. Instead of narrowing, the achievement gap in Kalamazoo had widened, casting a shadow over the once-hopeful program. Initially, the leaders of the organization overseeing the initiative staunchly defended their efforts, reluctant to acknowledge this unforeseen outcome. But as time passed, they embarked on a transformative journey of their own.

The organization extended an offer to those former Kalamazoo high school students from a decade ago, providing them with a second chance to utilize their college benefits under the Kalamazoo Promise. What unfolded was nothing short of captivating. Many students who had previously declined the opportunity now expressed a newfound interest. The program's terms remained unaltered; the metamorphosis had occurred within the hearts and minds of the students. Life had imparted valuable lessons, taking them on a journey of self-discovery, helping them discern their true passions and aspirations. Maturity had brought forth the realization of their existing skills and the gap between those skills and the skills they needed to thrive. These experiences had reshaped their perspectives and instilled in them a belief in the power of education.

It wasn't just the program's statistics and ideas that swayed the students to leverage the Kalamazoo Promise the second time around; it was the lessons the students learned and the perspectives they gained through years of facing real-world challenges. This revelation emphasized a profound truth: facts alone might not change our minds; it's the experiences we accumulate that truly mold our beliefs.

## Blind Spots

In our modern era dominated by the pervasive influence of social media, we've become acutely aware of how individuals with hidden agendas can expertly manipulate facts, whether it's to promote products or advance ideological interests. Simultaneously, we've also come to trust the expertise of professionals such as physicians and engineers. A puzzling question emerges: If we can both identify fraudsters and respect legitimate expertise, why do we sometimes willingly embrace false information and disregard indisputable facts?

In her illuminating article, "Why Facts Don't Change Our Minds," award-winning writer Elizabeth Kolbert (2017) sheds some light on the cognitive tendencies that shape our information processing and belief retention. These tendencies often lead to the creation of blind spots, which can undermine our best-laid plans and sometimes result in failures or worse outcomes. For starters, we possess a remarkable capacity to cling to our self-belief, even when confronted with evidence suggesting that our judgments may be flawed. This unwavering confidence in our reasoning abilities can inadvertently lead us to overlook the imperative need for self-reflection. In addition, our propensity for confirmation bias plays a profound role in our lives, as we naturally gravitate toward information that aligns with our existing beliefs. Although this innate inclination once aided in maintaining social cohesion, it now has the potential to distort our perception of factual reality. Understanding these cognitive idiosyncrasies helps us acknowledge the intricate challenges of altering our own perspectives or persuading others to do the same. It underscores the importance of engaging in discussions with empathy and open-mindedness, recognizing that presenting someone the facts alone may not suffice for reshaping their deeply ingrained convictions.

Furthermore, our readiness to identify flaws in others' arguments often surpasses our willingness to subject our own beliefs to the same level of scrutiny. We give ourselves a protective shield that impedes our ability to critically evaluate our viewpoints. Because humans are inherently social beings, our reasoning faculties have evolved more for negotiating group dynamics than for solitary analysis, occasionally prioritizing consensus-building or conflict avoidance over factual accuracy. That's why when addressing crucial matters, we should take into account the broader social context and remain mindful of how collective dynamics can influence our perceptions.

In essence, comprehending these cognitive tendencies invites us to approach the exchange of ideas with a sense of humility. It's not that you're necessarily thinking about things in a wrong or right way; rather, the issue often lies in thinking about them in only one way. We need to intentionally explore the limits of our own perspectives. This means actively seeking out alternative viewpoints and cultivating a deeper mindfulness about our own thought processes. By doing so, we open ourselves to a more comprehensive and nuanced understanding of the issues at hand.

In navigating the complexities of cognitive tendencies and the exchange of ideas, such traits as curiosity and openness to experience can serve as invaluable guides. Curiosity drives you to explore and seek new knowledge, essential for creative problem solving. The importance of maintaining an inquisitive mindset to nurture your curiosity is highlighted by how curiosity-driven approaches in learning environments lead to better outcomes. Similarly, openness to experience entails being receptive to new ideas, cultures, and perspectives, which will significantly enhance creative thinking. Embracing new experiences can broaden your creative horizons, as openness to experience is positively correlated with creative outputs. By embodying these traits, you not only deepen your understanding of the world but also cultivate a mindset conducive to innovation and growth.

## THINGS TO TRY

When engaging in discussions where you aim to change someone's mind, it's essential to approach the conversation with a blend of empathy and strategy. Here are a few actionable steps you can take to effectively influence others while respecting their perspectives:

### Focus on Social Aspects

Because reasoning is closely tied to social standing and relationships, frame your arguments in a way that respects others' social context and values. This can make your points more relatable and less threatening. To illustrate, when advocating for environmental sustainability to a group of people from an older generation who enjoy outdoor activities such as hunting and fishing, frame your arguments by emphasizing the importance of respect and our responsibility as stewards for our planet.

## Use More Than Just Facts

Simply providing facts may not be enough to change a belief, especially if it's deeply held. Combine factual information with storytelling or emotional appeals that resonate with the person's experiences and values. As a case in point, in a discussion about the benefits of organic farming, don't just present scientific data. Share a personal story about your own positive experiences with organic produce and how it improved your health. This will make the information more relatable to the person you're talking to.

## Be Patient and Empathetic

Changing deeply ingrained beliefs doesn't happen overnight. Be patient and empathetic in your approach, acknowledging the complexity and emotional attachment others might have to their beliefs. For example, if you have a friend with deeply entrenched political beliefs on the opposite side of the spectrum, don't try to change their views in one conversation. Engage in ongoing, respectful discussions over time, showing empathy and understanding for your friend's attachment to those beliefs.

# Facing the Facts

I've encountered very few individuals who truly grasp the concept that facts alone don't change minds. One such person was my mentor, Rob. He recruited me back from industry to academia and played a significant role in my professional development.

A few years after I'd established myself as an assistant professor, I embarked on a remarkable journey when my brother, my wife, and an office furniture company joined me in establishing an innovation center. This center found its home in an old photo lab conveniently situated across the street from the university. I entrusted the keys to this space to seven of the most innovative professors I knew, and the directive was clear: Focus solely on creative projects within the realm of innovation.

Soon enough, this innovation space became the nucleus of ground-breaking endeavors. It became the birthplace of innovation for the most esteemed student groups on campus, spanning engineering, medicine, and business. Even the governor recognized its potential, using the space to craft new policies alongside his cabinet. Renowned CEOs from the business world graced us with their presence, collaborating with their teams to produce celebrated innovations. Graduates who had apprenticed in this space ascended to prestigious positions in their careers.

Despite the undeniable success and impact of our innovation center, I encountered disbelief from university administrators when I sought their support. Given that they routinely showcased my work, their skepticism left me incredulous. It was then that I turned to Rob for guidance. Rob's words were carefully chosen and delivered with diplomacy, conveying the idea that bureaucracies, by their inherent design, prioritize stability and control, often at the expense of introducing new ideas or initiatives and their champions. His wisdom and experience helped me see the situation from a new perspective, aiding me in making sense of the paradoxical reaction of the administrators.

This clarity became crucial when I faced a pivotal moment in my career. An exciting opportunity emerged for me to potentially become the dean at one of the world's top universities. Following my interview for the position, I sought advice from Rob, a distinguished professor in the field. Behind closed doors, he laid out the unvarnished truth: deans primarily deal with fundraising, curriculum matters, and the challenges posed by faculty and students—areas where my strengths did not lie.

His warm smile accompanied this message, which resonated deeply within me. His insight went beyond the specific university context. Many large institutions will do anything to avoid variation. The most powerful change comes from us, from our own "self-authorizing behavior." I came to realize that academic deans, entrusted with the responsibility of steering and overseeing academic programs, frequently grappled with bureaucratic challenges and resistance to novel concepts. My proclivity for autonomous action, driven by a reluctance to seek prior approvals, often clashed with the traditional framework of an academic dean's role. Rob's gentle guidance reminded me that while I was precisely the right individual needed to nurture innovation beyond the boundaries of bureaucratic constraints, I would struggle in the position of dean since it did not align with my strengths.

Ultimately, this realization led me to make one of the most pivotal decisions of my career. I chose to forgo the dean position and remain at my university, but I no longer expected my school to fully recognize or support my work as an innovator. Instead, I found my motivation and joy in the creative work itself.

## THINGS TO TRY

When you're confronted with a reality or facts that you did not expect or realize, it's important for you to treat yourself with kindness and compassion. You need to put yourself in a space where you can open your mind and heart to a new reality—the bitter truth. Here are some practices that may help you lower your guard and learn from this experience.

### Navigate Skepticism and Success

Have you ever encountered skepticism or disbelief, despite undeniable success or innovation, similar to the experience with the innovation center that Jeff described? How did you navigate such situations, and what insights did you gain from those experiences?

### Embrace Autonomy and Innovation

Drawing from your reflections on past encounters, how might you apply the lessons learned to your current or future endeavors? Consider how you can embrace autonomy and champion innovation, even in the face of bureaucratic resistance or skepticism. What concrete steps can you take to nurture creativity and drive meaningful change within your sphere of influence?

# Uncommon Sense

The paradox of minds being resistant to change by facts alone reveals the complex interplay between facts and beliefs in shaping our perceptions and decisions. To understand this paradox, let us examine the concept of sensemaking, which emphasizes understanding how we interpret and assign meaning to our experiences. This involves grasping the emotional and social dimensions that underlie beliefs, recognizing our cognitive biases, and nurturing a paradoxical mindset.

The sensemaking process, deeply rooted in the works of organizational theorist Karl Weick (2000), involves a keen interpretation and understanding of the myriad events and scenarios you face in your professional environment. Weick's teachings underscore the significance of recognizing and navigating through the paradoxes that arise, such as by melding stability with change or aligning personal ambitions with collective objectives. This approach enables you to transform ambiguity into meaningful insights and see these contradictions not as mere obstacles but as catalysts for learning, decision-making, and growth, thus cultivating a resilient and evolving workplace.

The journey of sensemaking, as advocated by Karl Weick, intertwines seamlessly with the traits of curiosity and openness to experience. As you navigate the complexities of organizational dynamics, consider the importance of diversifying your data sources. Embrace the curiosity to explore beyond traditional avenues, engaging with employees, customers, and diverse work areas. By blending online research with in-person interactions, you open yourself to a wealth of perspectives, fostering a culture of continuous learning and exploration within your workplace.

Furthermore, collaboration becomes a cornerstone for insight when fueled by curiosity and openness. Engage with your colleagues in meaningful dialogues, leveraging their diverse insights to refine your understanding. Challenge stereotypes and outdated thinking, allowing each new perspective to guide you in developing innovative strategies and strengthening your flexibility in thinking. Embracing experimentation and narrative-driven communication gives you more data points that enhance your understanding of the situations unfolding before you. It can foster an environment that thrives on curiosity, adaptability, and growth. Through these actions, rooted in the principles of sensemaking, you cultivate a workplace that embraces the dynamic interplay between facts, beliefs, and experiences, continuously moving forward with resilience and evolution.

## THINGS TO TRY

To tap into your curiosity and openness to experience, here are three practical steps inspired by Karl Weick's

(2000) book *Making Sense of the Organization* that you can try:

## Diversify Your Data Sources

Expand your information-gathering tool kit. Go beyond the usual sources, such as financial reports. Engage with employees and customers, visit different work areas, and blend online research with in-person interactions. Look for disconfirming feedback. It will tell you if you're on the wrong track. By diversifying your sources, you open yourself up to a wealth of perspectives and insights that can fuel your curiosity and expand your understanding of the organization.

## Challenge Stereotypes

Break free from oversimplified assumptions. Instead of falling back on blanket statements like "All politicians are crooks," take the time to delve deeper into each unique situation. Embrace the complexity and nuance of individual circumstances, allowing yourself to see beyond stereotypes and cultivate a more open-minded approach to problem solving.

## Embrace New Perspectives

Resist the urge to apply outdated thinking to new situations. Instead, let each new context guide you in developing appropriate strategies. Embrace the opportunity to learn from different viewpoints and experiences, allowing yourself to adapt and evolve in response to changing circumstances. By embracing new perspectives, you can foster a culture of innovation and growth within yourself and your organization.

# Alternative Facts

Navigating the paradox of using facts to change minds involves tolerating the resistance that emotional beliefs present in the face of facts and embracing the reality that emotional beliefs often drive decisions. This requires a shift in our communication strategies by exploring the underlying emotional beliefs that drive resistance to facts and integrating both factual and emotional appeals in persuasive communication.

Consider the unsettling yet enlightening notion that there are lessons to be drawn from both cult leaders and world-builders—albeit with vastly different objectives.

Cult leaders, notorious for their ability to indoctrinate followers, understand a disturbing reality: facts are not the primary currency of persuasion. They delve deep into the psychology of human belief, and leverage emotions to create a compelling narrative that ensnares followers. Although we have no desire to emulate their harmful practices, we can extract valuable insights from their methods.

Now consider the world of fantasy fiction, a realm where such authors as J. R. R. Tolkien and George R. R. Martin wield their pens as world-builders. These masters of storytelling create intricate, immersive universes where facts are mere building blocks. They transport readers into these realms, inviting them to experience the story on a personal level by connecting with their emotions, values, and aspirations.

The common thread between these seemingly disparate worlds—cults and fantasy fiction—is the creation of an immersive experience. Cult leaders do it to manipulate minds, while world-builders do it to entertain and inspire. By examining these parallel paths, we can unearth the key to changing minds: it's not just about presenting facts; it's about crafting an experience that engages emotions, taps into deeply held values, and sparks the imagination. This is the power of narrative, which can be harnessed responsibly to influence others and broaden their perspectives, transcending the limitations of facts.

# Apply the Paradoxical Mindset Cycle: We Use Facts to Change Minds, but Minds Aren't Changed by Facts

Reflect on past experiences where you tried to change someone else's minds by presenting what you deemed to be solid, undeniable facts.

## Step 1: Find the Paradox

**Question to Answer:** When I tried to use facts to change someone else's opinion but failed to do so, what contradictions or inconsistencies did I see?

**Things to Do:** Identify moments where actions, decisions, or feelings clash with the rest of the narrative. Look for elements that feel out of place or confusing.

## Step 2: Analyze the Meaning

**Question to Answer:** What underlying factors and insights can I uncover by examining my tendency to rely on facts to change beliefs when emotions play a significant role?

**Things to Do:** Reflect on the facts and emotions to gain a deeper understanding of why the paradox exists and what it signifies.

## Step 3: Establish Guiding Principles

**Question to Answer:** What key learnings from my attempts to use facts to change minds can be turned into guiding principles for more effective persuasion?

**Things to Do:** Reflect on the insights you gain and identify specific aspects of those insights that can serve as actionable principles.

## Step 4: Implement Experiments

**Question to Answer:** What small, actionable changes can I implement based on my guiding principles to combine emotional and factual appeals in my communication?

**Things to Do:** Identify specific, manageable experiments; implement them; and reflect on their outcomes to refine your approach.

## PRACTICE THE FIRST PRINCIPLES: WE USE FACTS TO CHANGE MINDS, BUT MINDS AREN'T CHANGED BY FACTS

### Abundance of Ideas

Use diverse and creative approaches, such as storytelling and emotional appeals, to communicate your message, recognizing that multiple strategies beyond just presenting facts are often needed to effectively change minds.

### Flexibility in Thinking

Be willing to adapt your methods and perspectives, understanding that different people require different approaches, and that such adaptation can help bridge the gap between factual information and emotional belief systems.

### Risk-Taking

Take the risk of engaging in deeper, more personal conversations that go beyond facts, sharing your own experiences and vulnerabilities to connect on an emotional level and influence others more effectively.

## Curiosity

Develop a genuine curiosity about the beliefs and experiences of others, exploring why they hold certain views and how their personal stories shape their perspectives, which can inform your approach to changing their minds.

## Perseverance

Stay committed to the process of influencing change, even when your initial attempts fail, recognizing that changing deeply held beliefs takes time and sustained effort.

## Openness to Experience

Be open to new and varied experiences, both in how you present your arguments and in how you receive feedback, allowing these experiences to shape and refine your approach to influencing others.

## Self-Confidence

Maintain confidence in your ability to influence others, even when facts alone do not suffice, trusting in the power of your authentic and empathetic engagement to make a meaningful impact.

## CHAPTER 5

# We Set Goals for Change, but the Goals Change with the Change

**A** FEW WEEKS BEFORE THE 2010 rollout of the US Affordable Care Act, colloquially known as Obamacare, I received an unexpected request. A well-known former member of a presidential cabinet asked me to give a talk at a major event. Initially, I was hesitant. Throughout my career, I've steered clear of political entanglements, especially those that seemed more about rhetoric than substance. However, this group was interested in my expertise with large innovation ecosystems in health care, a topic I was deeply passionate about.

After some persuasion, I agreed to participate, but on my terms. I requested more than the standard eighteen-minute slot and the freedom to invite a panel of innovators from top global technology firms. To my surprise, the organizers agreed.

I curated a panel comprising heads of innovation from four of the world's most celebrated tech firms. My role was to moderate the discussion, a task I approached with a mix of excitement and trepidation. The health care debate in America was heated. On one side, proponents of a free market argued that universal access to health care stifled competition and created an artificial cost. On the other, advocates for a regulated market pointed to the disproportionate influence of large medical centers and pharmaceutical companies, accusing them of price-fixing.

As we prepared for the panel, it became clear that the future of health care wouldn't be determined by these traditional arguments. Both sides had powerful, well-funded constituencies influencing legislators, but both were overlooking a crucial factor: emerging technologies.

During the panel, held at the Kennedy Center in Washington DC, we explored groundbreaking innovations. We discussed how advanced diseases could be diagnosed in minutes using a cell phone, how rural health care could be revolutionized with mobile outpatient surgical vans, and how additive manufacturing could customize generic medicines at a low cost. These examples illustrated a future where medical care improved and costs decreased, independent of the actions of doctors, legislators, insurers, pharmaceutical companies, or lobbyists.

The real game changer was technology, a sector that, until then, hadn't been a major player in the health care debate. With technology, the issues of increasing access to health care and reducing costs could potentially be remedied through the use of mobile devices to diagnose patients and conduct some tests. It was becoming clear that the significant changes in health care would come from tech innovations, not from the traditional health care players or political maneuvering.

The discussion at the panel marked a shift in perspective. The tug-of-war over the future of health care, previously seen as a battle between free-market forces and political interest groups, was now being overtaken by the impact of emerging technologies. The incumbents, with their entrenched agendas, had failed to anticipate the transformative power of technology. They were unprepared for how the landscape of change was evolving.

The discussion shifted significantly because the panel was not affiliated with either the free-market or government-regulated perspectives; instead, the panelists embraced an innovation mindset—a third way. This was crucial for two reasons. First, those who rigidly adhered to one position often had strategic blind spots, falling into black-and-white thinking. Second, some who had vested interests were aware of the options, but aimed to obscure them from others. The panel's unbiased approach opened up new avenues for understanding and problem solving. While it did little to change the positions of the two lobbying groups, this new perspective highlighted their biases and limitations, revealing that their stances were not necessarily in the public's best interest. This approach underscored the importance of innovative thinking in fostering more inclusive and effective solutions, ultimately challenging the status quo and encouraging a broader, more balanced discourse.

What started as a debate on the direction of health care reform turned into a revelation about the nature of change itself. The rise of inexpensive, handheld technologies and the pervasive use of data were driving a transformation that traditional health care players and politicians could not. The change had changed, and those who couldn't adapt to the new reality were no longer the central drivers of this evolution.

In reflecting on the transformative power of technology in shaping the future of health care, it's crucial to acknowledge the distinct risk-taking culture of tech companies compared to the cultures of traditional health care entities. Tech firms are often more accustomed to taking risks, fueled by a culture where failure is not only accepted but also expected as a natural part of the innovation process. The degree of risk tolerance in the tech sector contrasts sharply with that in the health care sector, where failure can have life-or-death consequences and is consequently approached with more caution.

Moreover, the rapid and breakthrough successes experienced by tech companies instill a sense of confidence that traditional health care companies and medical centers may lack. These tech giants, accustomed to disrupting industries and pushing boundaries, approach health care innovation with a boldness and agility that can be both refreshing and unsettling to the more conservative health care establishment. This confidence, born of a track record of transformative innovation, further propels tech companies to explore new frontiers and challenge existing paradigms in health care delivery and management.

## Go with the Flow

The fluid nature of transformation is a concept deeply rooted in what is typically called process philosophy. This philosophical approach, tracing back to Heraclitus in ancient Greece and later expanded by Alfred North

Whitehead in the twentieth century, posits that reality is in constant flux—to paraphrase Heraclitus's famous saying, you cannot step into the same river twice. Building on Heraclitus's ideas, Whitehead (1929) further refined the notion, suggesting that life unfolds as a series of interconnected processes that constantly reshape our experiences.

In embracing this philosophical perspective, we are invited to recognize that change is not just an occasional occurrence but an essential and ongoing aspect of existence itself. It requires a profound understanding that everything in our world, from the physical environment to social structures to personal experiences, is in a perpetual state of evolution. Just as a river carves new paths through the landscape while also being shaped by its surroundings, our reality is shaped by the dynamic interactions and relationships among various elements.

Inherent in the philosophy of constant flux is the need for risk-taking and self-confidence. Embracing change means venturing into the unknown, stepping outside of our comfort zone, and challenging the status quo. It requires the courage to navigate uncertain waters, when we know that every decision carries the potential for both success and failure. Confidence plays a vital role in this process, as it empowers us to trust in our ability to adapt and thrive amid uncertainty. If we lack the will to take risks and the confidence to face the unknown, we are daunted at the prospect of embracing the dynamic nature of existence. However, by cultivating a mindset of boldness and self-assurance, we can harness the transformative power of change and navigate the ever-evolving currents of life with courage and resilience.

This perspective challenges the traditional notion of stability and encourages us to embrace the dynamic and fluid nature of life. It invites us to perceive reality not as a fixed and unchanging entity but as a vibrant and ever-evolving process. In doing so, we are prompted to approach our journey through life with a mindset of adaptability, resilience, and openness to the continuous flow of change. Ultimately, it suggests that by embracing the dynamic nature of existence, we can navigate the complexities of life with greater clarity, wisdom, and purpose.

# THINGS TO TRY

Through process philosophy, we can gain deeper understanding and appreciation of the complexity of life, change, and the beauty of little moments. Here are some practices that can push you to be more aware and open to the dynamics of change:

## Explore Interconnectedness in Everyday Life

Take time to notice the connections between seemingly unrelated events or phenomena in your daily experiences. Reflect on the ways that small changes in one area of your life can ripple out and affect other areas. By recognizing these interconnections, you'll gain a deeper understanding of the dynamic nature of reality.

## Embrace Flow and Change

Cultivate an awareness of the fluidity of life by observing natural processes and cycles, such as the changing seasons or the flow of water in a river. Practice being present in the moment and accepting the impermanent nature of all things. Allow yourself to let go of attachments to fixed outcomes and instead flow and work with the unfolding of events.

## Engage in Reflective Practices

Set aside time for introspection and contemplation, journaling about your experiences and insights. Consider how your beliefs and perceptions have evolved over time, and how you've adapted to various challenges and changes. By engaging in reflective practices, you'll deepen your understanding of the ongoing processes shaping your life, fostering a greater sense of connection to the broader world you live in.

# Seeing Is Not Believing

It started with a call from Matthias, the newly appointed head of inno-vation at a major German manufacturing company. He had breakthrough projects in need of funding from the executive team. Matthias invited me to facilitate an executive team meeting in Stuttgart. Unexpectedly, the executives hastily shifted the venue to a converted monastery near the French border, perhaps to safeguard their discussions from potential corporate espionage.

The company stood at a crossroads, confronted with a momentous decision: whether to make a substantial investment in an emerging market, a decision that would reroute existing profits toward future growth. Within the executive team, there was a rift. On one side stood the operating officers, fixated on profit and loss; on the other side, the senior innovation staff, charged with crafting technologies and marketing strategies to outshine their competitors.

The debates were fierce, with the pendulum of opinion swinging back and forth until, finally, the decision was reached—the company would invest. On the final day, the innovation teams unveiled their latest technologies and marketing initiatives. The executives were visibly impressed, but in the midst of these presentations, two seemingly minor details caught my keen eye.

First, the company had birthed numerous groundbreaking tech-nologies, but had consistently deferred integrating those innovations into new car models. This company was consistently the pioneer of development—from safety features that were now standard in budget-friendly cars to high-performance technologies found in luxury vehicles—yet it was the laggard in market entry. It was a culture that favored perfectionism over timely innovation.

Second, the company had undertaken a ride-sharing experiment in England. The results were nothing short of remarkable, but the company perceived the experiment as a mere branding tool. Matthias, however, perceived it differently. I shared the experiences of university students at my institution who, bereft of personal vehicles, were orchestrating shared rides through their smartphones. Their experience wasn't merely about sharing cars; it represented a transformation in the way people approached transportation. Matthias then proposed that the company could transition from being a mere car manufacturer to a mobility provider.

The idea garnered interest, but did not immediately translate into action. Despite the compelling evidence and visionary proposal, the executive team remained risk-averse. They were hesitant to deviate from their traditional business model, preferring instead to conduct more experiments and gather additional data before committing to such a significant shift. This cautious approach plunged the company into an endless cycle of planning and analysis, while rival firms seized the opportunity and swiftly capitalized on the emerging market of ride sharing. In the end, the executives' reluctance to embrace change left them trailing behind once again, watching as others reaped the rewards of bold innovation.

It wasn't until a few years later, when ride sharing began to surge in the US, that the significance of that meeting truly dawned on me. This company had once again pioneered innovation but had failed to capitalize on it. They had reached the future first, but had not recognized its potential.

Their aim had been to sell more cars, but this single-minded focus had blinded them to a burgeoning market. The irony was palpable. As ride sharing gained popularity, especially among the younger generation, who increasingly forgoes car ownership, the company missed the opportunity to spearhead a transformative shift in transportation.

This experience underscored a fundamental truth about change: our objectives must evolve with the shifting landscape. What starts as a clear goal can quickly become obsolete as new prospects and challenges emerge. In the realm of rapid innovation and ever-evolving consumer behaviors, the ability to adapt and redefine our goals is imperative.

# The Undiscovered Country

Developed by Columbia strategy professor Rita McGrath (2010), the concept of "discovery-driven planning" in her book *Discovery-Driven Growth: A Breakthrough Process to Reduce Risk and Seize Opportunity* offers a dynamic, real-time approach to strategic planning that transcends the traditional practice of setting and pursuing fixed objectives. It emphasizes continual learning, adaptation, and the reshaping of goals in response to evolving circumstances. This practical application of process philosophy demands paradoxical thinking and action, a recognition that rigid strategic plans quickly become obsolete in a constantly changing world. By prioritizing learning and flexibility, discovery-driven planning enables organizations to navigate uncertainty and seize emerging opportunities effectively.

Differing from conventional strategic planning, discovery-driven planning acknowledges the inherent uncertainty and unpredictability of the business landscape. It emphasizes continuous learning and adaptation, rather than striving for predetermined destinations. Organizations employing this approach focus on discovering opportunities and refining strategies iteratively based on real-world feedback. Furthermore, discovery-driven planning promotes experimentation and calculated risk-taking, with the understanding that innovation often requires venturing into uncharted territory. Embracing failure as a natural part of the learning process, organizations can rapidly iterate and refine their approach, ultimately increasing their perseverance and their chances of success in dynamic environments.

In today's rapidly changing world, the advantages of discovery-driven planning are evident. By remaining agile and adaptable, organizations can effectively respond to shifting market dynamics and emerging opportunities. Rather than being bound by rigid plans that quickly become outdated, they can proactively shape strategies based on real-time insights and feedback. This enhances their ability to capitalize on new opportunities while mitigating risks associated with uncertainty and disruption.

# THINGS TO TRY

To better prepare your voyage of discovery for unknown dangers in the seas ahead, consider these three action-able steps inspired by the principles of discovery-driven planning.

## Picture Your Success

Close your eyes and vividly envision what success looks like. See yourself achieving your aspirations, but remain open to the idea that this vision may evolve over time. By visualizing your desired outcome, you cultivate the confidence to take risks and the resilience to adapt to changing circumstances.

## Uncover Your Assumptions

Take a deep dive into the underlying beliefs that support your goals. Whether you're aiming for a career shift or a personal development milestone, examine what you believe must be true for your aspirations to succeed. Challenge these assumptions by engaging in conversations with industry experts or immersing yourself in relevant trends. This process builds confidence in your ability to navigate uncertainty and take calculated risks.

## Stay Flexible with Your Plans

As you gather insights and knowledge along your journey, be prepared to adjust your plans accordingly. Like a sailor adjusting their sails to catch the changing winds, embrace the necessity of shifting direction to make progress. Reflect regularly on your experiences, using moments of quiet contemplation to recalibrate and acknowledge your small victories. Embrace the idea that every misstep is an opportunity to learn and grow, guiding you toward your goals with greater wisdom and confidence.

# Simple Rules

In the face of a rapidly changing environment, we need to embrace a mindset that simplifies our approach to strategic decision-making. Taking inspiration from the article "Strategy as Simple Rules: How to Thrive in a Complex World" by Stanford management science professor Kathleen Eisenhardt and MIT business professor Donald Sull (2001), we can glean practical ways to handle the ever-evolving landscape of change.

Simple rules are essentials if you want to capture opportunities quickly in complex or chaotic situations. They are not hard lines that must be followed absolutely, but guidelines or rules of thumb that can help you negotiate challenging situations by quickly reminding you of some routes/solutions to work on. You can think of them as shortcuts in your brain to refer to a particular solution to a situation. Think of them like chess moves such as Ruy-Lopez or the Sicilian Defense.

What sets this strategy apart is its inherent flexibility. These uncomplicated rules decentralize decision-making, empowering both you and your team to act swiftly without the need for constant oversight, enhancing your openness to new experience. This autonomy and smart risk-taking breed agility, responsiveness, and perseverance, which are invaluable assets in a dynamic environment.

You can create different types of simple rules: how-to-rules, boundary rules, priority rules, timing rules, or exit rules. They need to be clear and specific, but also flexible. For example, you can create a boundary rules that you would only enter a partnership with another company with a particular culture or leadership style. This rule helps all your team members to naturally consider only those that fulfill the criteria as possible business partners.

# THINGS TO TRY

To infuse flexibility into your strategy, follow some practices here:

## Focus on Core Processes

Begin by zeroing in on the core processes that truly matter to your business, those critical few that have the most significant impact. This approach enables you to direct your attention and resources effectively, ensuring that you're investing where it counts the most. Next, create simple, guiding rules to steer these key processes. They are broad principles that empower you to make quick decisions—adaptable guidelines that provide the flexibility needed to navigate the unpredictable twists and turns of your environment.

## Align the Rules with Your Strengths

Harness these rules to align with your organization's unique strengths and differentiators. Tailor them to emphasize what sets you apart from the competition, ensuring that you stand out in the ever-evolving marketplace.

## Choose Wisely

Rules can also pile up easily as time goes by. Too numerous simple rules can also be overwhelming and confusing. So, review your simple rules on a regular basis and throw out the ones you don't need anymore.

## Adapt Your Rules

Be dynamic and responsive. Continuously refine and adapt your rules based on real-world experiences and feedback.

While these rules provide a guiding framework, they should also encourage creative problem solving and innovation within their boundaries. Think of them as a compass that continually adjusts its course in response to the shifting winds of change, guaranteeing that your plans remain both relevant and effective in an ever-changing landscape.

# Apply the Paradoxical Mindset Cycle: We Set Goals for Change, but the Goals Change with the Change

Reflect on an experience where you set goals in a change endeavor and then the circumstances changed as you moved forward.

## Step 1: Find the Paradox

**Question to Answer:** Where do I notice contradictions, inconsistencies, or illogical parts in my experiences when the goals I set for change evolve as the change itself occurs?

**Things to Do:** Identify moments where actions, decisions, or feelings clash with the rest of the narrative. Look for elements that feel out of place or confusing.

## Step 2: Analyze the Meaning

**Question to Answer:** What underlying factors and insights can I uncover by examining the paradox of setting goals that shift in response to the changing nature of the change process?

**Things to Do:** Reflect on the facts and emotions to gain a deeper understanding of why the paradox exists and what it signifies.

## Step 3: Establish Guiding Principles

**Question to Answer:** What key learnings from my experience of evolving goals can be turned into guiding principles to help me adapt and thrive amid continual change?

**Things to Do:** Reflect on the insights you've gained and identify specific aspects of those insights that can serve as actionable principles.

## Step 4: Implement Experiments

**Question to Answer:** What small, actionable changes can I implement based on my guiding principles to better align my goals with the dynamic nature of change and improve my adaptability?

**Things to Do:** Identify specific, manageable experiments; implement them; and reflect on their outcomes to refine your approach.

# PRACTICE THE FIRST PRINCIPLES: WE SET GOALS FOR CHANGE, BUT THE GOALS CHANGE WITH THE CHANGE

### Abundance of Ideas

Regularly brainstorm new approaches and alternatives to achieve your goals, understanding that flexibility and adaptability are key as your objectives evolve with changing circumstances.

### Flexibility in Thinking

Embrace the need to continually adjust your strategies and expectations, allowing your goals to naturally evolve in response to new insights and developments.

## Risk-Taking

Be willing to take calculated risks as your goals shift, recognizing that stepping into the unknown can lead to innovative solutions and breakthroughs.

## Curiosity

Maintain a curious mindset about the changing landscape, constantly seeking to understand new trends and factors that might influence the evolution of your goals.

## Perseverance

Stay committed to your overall vision, even as specific goals change, understanding that persistence is crucial in negotiating the dynamic nature of change.

## Openness to Experience

Welcome new experiences and perspectives that arise as your goals shift, using these opportunities to refine and enhance your strategies.

## Self-Confidence

Trust in your ability to adapt and succeed despite the shifting goals, reinforcing your confidence in your capacity to manage and thrive amid ongoing change.

## CHAPTER 6

# We Try to Minimize Conflict, but Change Is Created by It

I WAS BROUGHT IN TO CONSULT with one of the world's leading corporations, a massive conglomerate with over twenty divisions that were the revenue darlings of Wall Street. Among the company's holdings were several television networks and movie studios. My mission was clear: I had to find ways to help local TV stations increase their revenue, especially since local ad buys were steadily declining.

The man who brought me into the company, the head of local TV programming, was named Tom. A seasoned professional with a deep understanding of the industry, Tom had reservations about the future of local TV stations.

Our journey began in Chicago, where we gathered to develop an innovation strategy. A few months later, we held a jumpstart event in Ann Arbor, bringing together most of the station managers to brainstorm creative solutions and ways to test them in each of their markets. Conflicting interests came into play. The pressing need to show immediate revenue clashed with the long-term goal of developing scalable and sustainable solutions. Many promising ideas were rejected before they even had a chance to be tested.

During one particularly frustrating meeting, I remember emphasizing to the group, "The worst of all growth strategies is an increasing share of a decreasing market." They reluctantly nodded in agreement, understanding the harsh reality.

With the group exhausted, depleted, and at a standstill, I sought input from three students I had enlisted to assist with the logistics of the jumpstart event. We asked them what programs and stations they watched. To our astonishment, they revealed that they didn't own a television; they watched streamed content on their computers. At the time, the technology and bandwidth for streaming were still in their infancy, and these students were accessing content from sources assumed to be outside conventional intellectual property laws.

Despite initial resistance from the station managers, we decided to experiment with using streaming technology to support the local TV stations' revenue strategies, akin to how newspapers initially transitioned from physical to digital versions. Two companies, one focused on technology and the other on retail sales, were the first to venture into this emerging space.

I discussed the experiments with Sandra, a senior VP. She found the concept intriguing, but believed that progress would be too slow because the station managers lacked the expertise and motivation to move forward rapidly and expansively.

Sandra collaborated with the senior VP of finance to create a new business—one that exclusively streamed top-quality content, often directly competing with the local TV stations. It was a bold move that was met with a lot of resistance from the station managers.

Sandra then hired Layla, a young and enterprising technology program director from an online retail company, to lead the effort. Layla insisted on hiring her own staff and working in a hidden location without interference from Sandra, Tom, or anyone else.

The transformation was marked by continuous contention. Tom was stretched thin dealing with fierce resistance and anger from the station managers. Sandra grappled with the challenge of justifying the substantial costs of the new streaming service to the executive team, who were demanding proof of its high profitability. Meanwhile, Layla felt the mounting pressure from Sandra to adhere to an aggressive timeline, further adding to the tense atmosphere surrounding the project.

As the months passed, the corporation's leadership began to grow nervous, as the new venture was taking nearly a year to develop. When the streaming service finally debuted, it was groundbreaking. An impressive array of digital programs was available on demand, accompanied by limited commercials, which could be eliminated with a subscription fee.

The new network became a massive success. It's important to mention, however, as is often the case with pioneering ventures, that competitors soon followed, investing substantial resources in marketing their networks. Being the first to enter the market didn't guarantee staying ahead for long. Moreover, the transition to streaming, as expected, came with significant switching costs and initial losses, primarily due to declining advertising revenues. Over time, local TV stations added online streaming services to complement their traditional broadcasts, which eventually evolved into apps. While these apps generated new advertising revenue, it took years before they could fully offset the steep losses the local station owners faced from dwindling broadcast advertising. There was no fairy-tale ending: given the declining revenues, the company eventually sold its local television stations to another conglomerate, which also struggled to make money in the new reality of online streaming. Tom moved on and secured an executive position, as did some of the station managers, while many retired and others struggled to adjust to the shift in their careers.

Tom's and Sandra's flexibility in thinking and openness to experience played crucial roles in the success. Rather than stubbornly sticking to set plans, they remained receptive to unconventional ideas, even when they initially seemed daunting. This adaptability allowed them to navigate challenges effectively, demonstrating the importance of maintaining an open mind when confronted with complex situations.

## The Loyal Opposition

Sociologist Mary Parker Follett's (1924) pioneering work on "constructive conflict" revolutionized our understanding of organizational dynamics and its implications for creative and paradoxical thinking. Follett emphasized that conflict, when managed constructively, can lead to innovation and growth within organizations. Instead of viewing conflict as inherently negative, Follett advocated for embracing it as a catalyst for exploring diverse perspectives and generating innovative solutions. By fostering an environment where conflicting ideas are welcomed and synthesized, organizations can harness the power of creative tension to adapt and thrive in rapidly changing environments. Follett's insights continue to inspire modern approaches to leadership and problem solving, high-lighting as they did the transformative potential of constructive conflict in fostering creative and paradoxical thinking. Follett articulated these ideas in her book *Creative Experience* a hundred years ago(!), solidifying her legacy as a pioneer in organizational theory.

There are numerous illustrative examples of Follett's observations on the creative power of diverse mindsets. John Lennon, drawing from the well of his Liverpool upbringing, crafted the song "Strawberry Fields Forever," a mirror to his soul. This was not just an individual act of creativity; it was a catalyst that sparked Paul McCartney's creative response. McCartney, revisiting his own memories but viewing them through a different prism, composed "Penny Lane." Their songs, though rooted in the same geographic and emotional landscapes, were reflections through different points of view. Theirs was a dynamic interplay of differing perspectives, a dance of creative tension that led to some of the most enduring music of their era.

Their story underscores a crucial lesson: when organizations or partnerships embrace the energy of conflict, channeling it into creative and constructive avenues, they don't just survive—they thrive. Lennon and McCartney's partnership, fueled by their individual differences and mutual respect, became a driving force in their groundbreaking musical journey.

This phenomenon of "opposites attracting" in creative partnerships is not unique to Lennon and McCartney. It's a pattern seen in various fields, from technology to finance. Consider the synergy between Steve Jobs and Steve Wozniak at Apple, where Jobs's flair for design and marketing complemented Wozniak's technical prowess. Then there's the partnership of Warren Buffett and Charlie Munger, where Buffett's investment strategies were enriched by Munger's broader business insights. In each case, these pairs thrived on their differences, leveraging them to drive innovation and change.

The death of an organization isn't typically marked by conflict; it's marked by apathy. Conflict signifies energy, action, and care—it's a sign of life. When an organization stops fighting, it means that nothing matters anymore. Therefore, we want to allow for opposing opinions or opposing leaders to appear at the scene. Great leaders, especially those who change the world, often emerge in pairs. A prime example is the story of Lennon and McCartney, a compelling case study of how creative friction can be a force for innovation. Their partnership is a testament to the transformative energy of creative conflict.

## THINGS TO TRY

To harness and prosper from the creative power of constructive conflict, consider these approaches:

### Seek a Complementary Partner

Identify someone whose abilities and viewpoints contrast with yours. Look for individuals who bring diverse skills, backgrounds, or perspectives to the table. This diversity lays the foundation for a robust, creative alliance, fostering flexibility in thinking and openness to new experiences. Embrace the opportunity to learn from each other's strengths and differences, as doing so can lead to more innovative solutions and approaches.

### Foster a Healthy Competition

Cultivate a dynamic of friendly rivalry with your partner to mutually inspire and elevate your collective endeavors. Set shared goals or challenges that encourage both of you to push your boundaries and explore new possibilities. A healthy competitive spirit not only fuels motivation but also fosters continuous improvement and growth. By challenging each other to excel, you reinforce your paradoxical mindset and drive toward innovation.

## Engage in Regular Feedback

Establish a routine of sharing and critiquing each other's work. This continuous exchange can sharpen your ideas and bolster your joint creative output. By providing constructive feedback and actively seeking input from your partner, you create a collaborative environment conducive to growth and innovation. Embracing regular feedback helps refine your thinking, refine your ideas, and ultimately enhance the quality of your collaborative work.

# Voice of Judgment

Early in my career, I found myself as an executive in the world's fastest-growing food company. My role was to develop innovations that would revolutionize speedy food delivery. As the first PhD hire in the company, I was given unprecedented freedom to experiment. However, my innovations, though eventually setting industry standards, initially met resistance from franchisees who saw them as diverging from short-term company goals and leading to increasing costs.

I was used to conflict being the norm. I was accustomed to working through conflict to create amazing solutions, even with my most vehement detractors. The clashes, the debates, the heated arguments—these were all part of the process of change. And I thrived in that environment.

Decades later, as a seasoned professional, I was approached by

Larry, the chief operating officer of one of the world's largest food companies. They needed help in encouraging their franchisees to embrace innovation while maintaining consistent revenues. This challenge mirrored the paradox I had navigated in my early career. Yet when I met with these franchisees, I was unexpectedly confronted with unresolved feelings from my past experiences. I found myself particularly frustrated because this group was not succeeding, and instead of recognizing their failures and seeking a path to improvement, they seemed to have adopted a negative attitude, rejecting any new ideas.

As the sessions progressed, my inability to manage these emotions became evident. My approach, tainted by a sense of superiority and condescension, hindered effective communication. By the third session, it was clear that my involvement was more a hindrance than a help, and I was politely dismissed. This was a low point in my career. It took me weeks to accept that my failure came from my inability to engage constructively with the franchisees.

Despite my past successes in navigating conflict, I found myself unable to transcend my own dominant worldview when confronted with franchisees resistant to innovation. In a way, their intractable thinking resembled my own. Thinking isn't just rational; it's also emotional, and neither they nor I were ready to work through our feelings.

This experience was a profound lesson in humility and the importance of self-awareness. My inner dialogue of judgment had not only clouded my perception but also directly impacted my professional effectiveness. It was my job to help the franchisees get to the next place, and, unfortunately, I failed. This incident served as a stark reminder that success in change efforts requires not just technical expertise but also the ability to empathetically and respectfully collaborate with others, regardless of past experiences or preconceived notions.

Looking back, I now understand that sometimes the biggest impediment to change is not external resistance but our own internal biases and preconceptions. It's a lesson I carry with me as I continue to work in the ever-evolving world of innovation and change management.

# Ambidextrous Mindset

In our book *The Innovation Code: The Creative Power of Constructive Conflict* (DeGraff & DeGraff, 2017), we explore the dynamic role of "ambidextrous-mindset" in leaders who adeptly manage difference and disagreement within their organizations. These leaders understand that conflict, typically seen as a negative force, can actually foster significant growth and innovation when approached constructively. The key lies not in the mere existence of differing viewpoints but in the effective management and integration of these perspectives to fuel progress. By embracing and harnessing these conflicts, leaders can unlock a wealth of groundbreaking ideas and solutions, transforming potential road-blocks into opportunities for innovation. Central to leveraging this para-dox effectively is the cultivation of an ambidextrous mindset among leaders and teams. This mindset involves not only recognizing but actively seeking out and integrating diverse perspectives into a unified strategy. It entails viewing the varied strengths and weaknesses of team members not as opposing forces but as complementary components of a cohesive whole.

True diversity in teams extends beyond superficial traits to include a rich mix of expertise, beliefs, and experiences. Such diversity creates a robust mosaic of viewpoints, enhancing the team's resilience and capacity for innovative problem solving. Moreover, mastering the art of constructive engagement in conflicts is essential for transforming potential challenges into opportunities for improvement. Viewing con-flict through this lens allows teams to use disagreements as a foundation for deeper understanding and for generating innovative solutions. It is vital, however, that the focus on the overarching vision or goal remains steadfast. Amid the diverse and often conflicting approaches and opinions, a shared commitment to common objectives ensures that all efforts are aligned and purpose driven, thereby maintaining coherence and motivation within the team.

This philosophy of embracing and resolving conflicts constructively is particularly pertinent in today's rapidly changing business environ-ment. Ambidextrous leaders thrive by facilitating an atmosphere where debate and difference are not just tolerated but encouraged as methods to deeper insight and superior outcomes. In such environments, conflicts are reframed as opportunities to question the status quo and to innovate beyond conventional boundaries. This dynamic can often lead to the development of novel products, services, and processes that might never have been conceived in a more harmonious but less challenging atmosphere.

The effectiveness of this approach hinges on the ability of leaders to cultivate a culture of open communication and mutual respect. Within such a culture, individuals feel valued and heard, making them more willing to contribute their unique ideas and feedback. This openness fosters a deeper level of trust among team members, which is crucial for navigating the complexities of conflict without succumbing to dysfunction or fragmentation. As teams learn to engage in healthy, constructive conflict, they build a shared resilience and adaptability, becoming more adept at responding to external pressures and changes. The paradox of conflict as a catalyst for growth and innovation is a powerful tool in the hands of ambidextrous leaders, driving innovation and sculpting a resilient organizational culture poised to meet future challenges.

## THINGS TO TRY

There are four steps for harnessing conflict constructively and transforming it into creative solutions:

### Assemble a Diversity of Perspectives

Enhance diversity by bringing together individuals with different backgrounds and expertise. Encourage sharing of unique insights through brainstorming sessions across various departments. Focus on convening people who can generate various ideas that challenge conventional thinking and foster innovation, not just fulfilling diversity quotas.

### Engage in the Conflict

Cultivate a culture where differing opinions are valued. Establish guidelines for respectful discussion and offer conflict resolution training. Encourage open expression of dissenting opinions in meetings, where team members focus on issues rather than personal differences.

### Establish a Shared Vision or Goal

Clearly communicate the team's shared vision and involve members in goal-setting so as to promote better engagement. Reinforce these objectives through team-building activities and regular meetings, showing how each member's work contributes to these goals. Use common goals to guide conflict resolution, keeping the team aligned and focused.

### Construct Hybrid Solutions

Foster a culture of experimentation to develop hybrid solutions. Implement an iterative approach with continuous cycles of testing, feedback, and refinement. Use pilot projects to test new ideas, then adapt based on feedback. Celebrate successes and be open about challenges, as both are crucial to the iterative process of innovation.

## Challenge Accepted

Change is often driven by constructive conflict, a concept that can initially seem counterintuitive. Many people prefer efficiency through agreement and alignment, avoiding conflicts that might slow down progress. However, embracing constructive conflict is essential because it produces generative energy and hybrid ideas, which are necessary to create genuine buy-in for substantial change. Further, integrating the paradoxical mindset traits of flexibility in thinking and openness to experience enhances the process.

Instead of avoiding conflict to maintain harmony, consider it as a catalyst for innovation and growth. Conflict, when approached with open-mindedness and respectful communication, can lead to innovative solutions, fresh perspectives, and positive transformation. Flexibility in thinking allows for the exploration of diverse viewpoints, while openness to experience encourages receptivity to new ideas and perspectives.

Conflict serves as a crucible for refining your personal goals and organizational strategies. Instead of shying away from conflicts, view them as opportunities to challenge and strengthen your ideas. Collaborating with others and addressing conflicts directly can lead to creative and effective solutions, benefiting both personal growth and organizational success.

Change often brings unexpected challenges, making adaptability and resilience crucial. Embracing constructive conflict helps you and your organization become more flexible, capable of navigating the twists and turns that change presents. Flexibility in thinking enables you to adapt to evolving circumstances, while openness to experience fosters a willingness to explore new approaches and solutions.

Your journey of personal and organizational change encompasses not just your personal goals but also your interactions with others and the world around you. Seek out diverse perspectives and experiences, letting them shape your path and your organization's direction in practical ways. Embrace the interconnectedness of personal growth, relationships, and aspirations, as well as organizational progress.

Adopt the practice of welcoming differences and constructive conflicts, thereby allowing new ideas, interactions, and experiences to blend together, creating a dynamic palette of possibilities. Just as individuals collaborate to create something unique and meaningful, let the fusion of ideas and constructive conflicts enable you and your organization to navigate change effectively and achieve your goals with richness and originality. Flexibility in thinking and openness to experience enrich the collaborative process, facilitating the emergence of innovative solutions and adaptive strategies.

# Apply the Paradoxical Mindset Cycle: We Try to Minimize Conflict, but Change Is Created by It

Reflect on an experience in which you tried to avoid or resolve conflicts during a period of change.

## Step 1: Find the Paradox

**Question to Answer:** Where do I notice contradictions, inconsistencies, or illogical parts in my efforts to minimize conflict, despite knowing that conflict can drive change and innovation?

**Things to Do:** Identify moments where actions, decisions, or feelings clash with the rest of the narrative. Look for elements that feel out of place or confusing.

## Step 2: Analyze the Meaning

**Question to Answer:** What underlying factors and insights can I uncover by examining my attempt to avoid conflict when it can lead to constructive and creative outcomes?

**Things to Do:** Reflect on the facts and emotions to gain a deeper understanding of why the paradox exists and what it signifies.

## Step 3: Establish Guiding Principles

**Question to Answer:** What key learnings from my experiences with conflict can be turned into guiding principles that will help me harness it constructively for change and innovation?

**Things to Do:** Reflect on the insights you've gained and identify specific aspects of those insights that can serve as actionable principles.

### Step 4: Implement Experiments

**Question to Answer:** What small, actionable changes can I implement based on my guiding principles to better embrace and manage conflict, turning it into a catalyst for positive change and innovation?

**Things to Do:** Identify specific, manageable experiments; implement them; and reflect on their outcomes to refine your approach.

## PRACTICE THE FIRST PRINCIPLES: WE TRY TO MINIMIZE CONFLICT, BUT CHANGE IS CREATED BY IT

### Abundance of Ideas

Encourage a variety of ideas and solutions during conflicts, recognizing that the clash of different perspectives can lead to creative breakthroughs and innovative changes.

### Flexibility in Thinking

Be open to adjusting your viewpoints and strategies in response to conflict, understanding that adaptability can turn disagreements into opportunities for growth and improvement.

### Risk-Taking

Embrace the risk of engaging in and addressing conflicts head-on, knowing that confronting issues directly can lead to meaningful and transformative changes.

## Curiosity

Approach conflicts with a curious mindset, seeking to understand the underlying causes and perspectives involved, which can uncover new insights and drive constructive change.

## Perseverance

Persist through conflicts and challenges, recognizing that enduring and working through disagreements are often necessary to achieve significant and lasting change.

## Openness to Experience

Be open to the experiences and lessons that come from engaging in conflict, using these interactions to learn, grow, and evolve your approaches to change.

## Self-Confidence

Maintain confidence in your ability to navigate and resolve conflicts, trusting that your skills and resilience will help you transform discord into positive outcomes.

# We Attempt to Avoid Failure, but All Learning Is Developmental and Requires Failure

T HE STOCK PRICE WAS PLUNGING, and the failures were splashed across the cover of the top business magazines when Miriam's office reached out to me. The beverage company had always been regarded as one with the best marketing campaigns, with a storied history that had made it a darling of Wall Street. But after dominating its niche for over a century, it unexpectedly found itself in a bit of a predicament.

Stable with predictable revenue growth, this company had been a sure bet for investors. Its charismatic CEO, Antonio, had built the modern version through aggressive acquisition of global brands. Everything changed after Antonio passed. The CEO who followed him, Christopher, had an impressive track record for marketing and brand management, but his clever maneuvering with international tax laws and questionable management practices led to his forced departure after just a couple of years.

Martin, the successor to Christopher, was tasked with restoring order and profitability to the company. While he successfully focused on international growth and diversified the product offering to include health beverages, his strategy was to stay the course, essentially minimizing any significant change.

Miriam, the new head of strategy, had a proven track record of developing new products and significantly increasing revenues in Asia. She had been brought back to the home office to implement a new innovation strategy within the innovation ecosystem she was building.

I was brought in to help develop innovation leaders capable of thriving under Miriam. It all began with a meeting in a rural resort far from the corporate world's beaten path. We stayed in rustic cottages and held our meetings in an old-fashioned meetinghouse.

The company's leaders were clearly concerned about the plummeting share price and their job security, so there was little willingness to embrace new things. However, as the weeks went by and particularly when the senior executives weren't present, the leaders began to slowly unveil their failures, past and present.

One leader, Pete, reached out to me for help with a failing product. It was a beverage packaged in an aluminum bottle, a first-of-its-kind creation, featuring a zero-calorie sweetener that tasted just like sugar, along with nutraceuticals to enhance its health benefits. The company positioned it as a coffee-like drink at a premium price point, which was a bold strategy. Unfortunately, sales were dismal, and the company was on the verge of discontinuing the product.

I was intrigued because this was a genuine innovation, the first I had seen from the company in years. Yet they didn't know how to handle its failure. Pete explained that they had conducted extensive marketing research, just as they did for all their products, so the slow sales had caught them off guard.

I told Pete that the product was remarkable, but that they had entered the market a bit too early and didn't target the right market. We needed to accelerate the failure cycle to quickly find its real market—the first-mover consumers who would embrace this type of beverage. Essentially, the company didn't understand the product it had created, a product that presented an opportunity for profound change within the company, from top to bottom. Pete and I worked to launch several cycles of quick experiments in several countries in Europe, adjusting the product and its marketing plan after each cycle. Lo and behold, after a few experiments, we found the right market for the product. It was new, still small, but growing rapidly.

Regrettably, but unsurprisingly given the company's intolerance of risk-taking and a lack of appetite to do something new, the company decided to play it safe and stick to its usual practices when it was time to scale and distribute the new drink around the world. The company ended up eliminating most of the product's true innovations: it switched to a traditional plastic bottle, replaced the new sweetener with the old one, removed the nutraceuticals, and sold it in grocery stores just like its other products.

Ironically, that small new market that the company had initially penetrated with an innovative new product, only to later forsake for a more conventional product and market, ultimately burgeoned into a very lucrative opportunity. However, when it finally reentered this market with a revamped strategy and product, the company found the market saturated with competitors. The company had forfeited its first mover advantage in the market. Its revulsion of failure and of the new essentially constrained its own growth. Eventually, the company adapted not out of choice but out of necessity in order to remain competitive in this dynamic market landscape.

The entire ordeal left Miriam deeply disappointed, especially since she had been passed over for the CEO position, and she moved on to a different company that was more willing to embrace her breakthrough strategy and to weather the storm of failures along the way.

As for me, I left with Miriam, fully aware that companies that boast about change are often reluctant to endure the failures that ultimately pave the way for successes.

## Accelerating Failure

Real change involves stepping into the unknown and embracing the inevitability of failures—whether in personal endeavors or organizational shifts—as part of the learning process. Consider the process of learning to play the piano: it begins with basic skills, such as reading notes and recognizing pitches; progresses through mastering simple to complex tunes; and culminates in creating and improvising music. This journey is punctuated by repetitive practice and numerous mistakes, underscoring that real mastery arises not from avoiding failure but from leveraging these experiences to foster rapid learning and improvement.

When we apply this concept to broader scenarios, we realize that smooth, uninterrupted change often indicates only incremental progress or a mere extension of current practices. True expertise in one area does not guarantee competence across other fields, as skills are often specific to particular domains. For instance, an excellent doctor may not necessarily excel as a public speaker. Real growth, therefore, requires more than just good fortune or isolated expertise; it demands a willingness to engage with challenges and learn from setbacks.

Thomas Davenport's (2009) essay "How to Design Smart Business Experiments" delves into this theme, highlighting the critical role of structured experimentation in business. Davenport, an information technologist at Babson College, articulates the counterintuitive notion that while our instincts drive us to shun failure, significant development and learning necessitate facing and learning from these failures. He champions the use of scientific principles in business experiments to convert failures into learning opportunities with valuable insights. These experiments, crucial for innovation and effective decision-making, challenge traditional, extensive planning approaches that can stifle action and adaptability.

The practice of accelerating the failure cycle is crucial for innovation, for it advocates for small, swift experiments that offer crucial insights and allow for agile responses to new challenges. This approach minimizes the cost and impact of failures, transforming potential setbacks into vital learning moments. Such a proactive embrace of failure not only speeds up the learning process but also fosters more robust and adaptive strategies, paving the way for sustained innovation and success.

# THINGS TO TRY

To effectively implement and sustain change, try these three critical action steps that encompass planning, implementing, analyzing, executing, and cultivating a culture supportive of continuous experimentation and learning:

## Initiate and Plan Your Experiment

Begin by refining an innovative idea that promises potential economic benefits and presents a clear, actionable path forward. Plan an experiment by determining the optimal number of test and control groups necessary to ensure that the results will be reliable. Use simulations to fine-tune the approach, and be ready to extend the testing period if data variations warrant further investigation.

## Implement, Document, and Analyze

Introduce your idea on a small scale to monitor its effectiveness and gather feedback, making necessary adjustments before wider implementation. Document each phase meticulously, organizing the findings for easy access and analysis. Use tools to analyze the data from multiple sites, checking for statistically significant outcomes. This detailed analysis may highlight the need for additional testing to refine the approach.

## Execute and Cultivate a Culture of Experimentation

Ensure clear and consistent communication with all stakeholders and adapt your plan based on feedback and external factors. Adjust management practices as necessary based on the impacts of the tests. Promote a culture that values evidence-based decision-making and accountability, equipping team members with the resources to conduct thorough experiments. Encourage senior management to support an experimentation mindset, emphasizing the importance of well-informed strategies for sustainable success.

## Too Good to Be True

Jim, the VP of marketing for an American multinational conglomerate, approached me with a critical mission: orchestrating a decisive strategy conference. Our task? To determine the destiny of a line of micromesh medical tubing known as stents. Should the company invest or divest? The health care division of Jim's organization stood at a crossroads, grappling with years of stagnant growth in the stent business.

Over the past decade, the stent industry had witnessed two game-changing innovations: the drug-eluting stent and the bare-metal stent. While nimble niche players swiftly embraced these advancements, Jim sought a more informed path forward. Given the unparalleled market reach and cost-efficient stent-manufacturing capabilities of this corporate titan, Jim identified and seized an opportunity.

We assembled twenty-one physicians from various corners of the nation, representing diverse health care realms—esteemed medical centers, modest private practices, and expansive HMO networks. Our plan was to envision three distinct scenarios for the future of US health care: capitated costs, technology-driven revolutions, and the status quo.

The physicians, divided into different groups based on their professional interest, skills, and specialties, engaged in exhaustive debates to craft and exchange insights on stent requisites tailored to each scenario. Our dedicated teams in marketing and product development meticulously documented every concern and potential solution. Then we gathered the product developers, who explored materials, potential innovations, and prospective products to navigate the ever-evolving health care landscape.

When the conference concluded, the physicians returned to their homes, leaving Jim and me submerged in weeks of planning and reporting. Our next move was to enlist a distinguished consulting firm, specializing in due diligence, to conduct an exhaustive analysis of the recommendations. The results held promise, particularly the concept of making significant marketing investments to secure a commanding market share. When the executive team received the results, they expressed reservations and concerns, but allocated a modest budget for Jim to run limited, focused experiments to validate the reinvestment recommendations.

Months passed, and to my surprise, Jim ceased returning my calls. Almost a year passed without contact. When he reappeared, he unveiled an unexpected outcome. The experiments had yielded astonishing results, prompting the executive decision to sell the stent business to a medical device corporation with a robust portfolio of vascular and renal prosthesis devices. The acquiring company was impressed with the market strategy we crafted and the proven viability of the updated stent.

In a twist of irony, Jim's company, despite conducting the experiments, hadn't mustered enough faith in their findings to reinvest in the advanced technology. While they did secure a profit from the sale, it paled in comparison to the meteoric forecasts meant to convince the company to embrace the advanced technology.

Even more confounding, the same hesitancy plagued the medical device company that acquired Jim's stent business. Despite exhaustive experiments, testing, and in-depth analytics, this second company didn't adhere to the due diligence recommendations regarding the level of investment. A competitor, having invested in their version of an advanced stent, recognized the possibilities and committed substantial resources, eventually surpassing the market share of the medical device giant. And so, in a double twist of irony, it was this third company that fully grasped the potential of Jim's experiments. They comprehended the risks and rewards of failure, wholeheartedly embracing the opportunity to capture and dominate the stent market.

# Games People Play

In his book *Finite and Infinite Games*, religion and history scholar James Carse (2011) introduces a thought-provoking dichotomy in understanding human endeavors and interactions: finite and infinite games. Finite games are those with defined rules, players, and objectives, and they end when a player has won or the objective has been achieved. This concept can be applied to specific change initiatives, whether they address personal goals or organizational transformations. In these scenarios, success is measured by the achievement of a predetermined outcome, and failure is often seen as not reaching the set goal, marking the end of that particular game. Think of chess as an example of a finite game. In the end, there is a winner and loser.

By contrast, infinite games are ongoing, with rules and objectives that evolve over time. Each effort is part of a continuous process of development and adaptation, and failure is not a definitive end. Instead, failure is an integral part of the learning journey—an opportunity to gather insights, develop new strategies, and enhance capabilities. This approach to change emphasizes the importance of resilience and flexibility, encouraging a mindset that perceives the journey of change to be as significant as the destination. In infinite games, the ultimate aim is not to win in the traditional sense but to perpetuate growth, learning, and adaptation. Consider how a debate with a colleague might be viewed as an infinite game. The back-and-forth will continue as long as the participants agree to play on.

In her article "Strategies for Learning from Failure," Harvard business professor Amy C. Edmondson (2011) explores the intricacies of failure within organizations, emphasizing that failure is not inherently negative but instead a crucial opportunity for learning and improvement. She identifies common misconceptions that hinder effective learning from failures, such as the simplistic belief that asking employees to reflect on their mistakes will prevent future errors. Instead, Edmondson proposes that organizations adopt a more nuanced understanding of failure, recognizing it as sometimes bad, sometimes inevitable, and sometimes beneficial.

Edmondson argues that the real challenge lies in changing the organizational culture to view failures as a source of valuable learning. This requires creating a psychologically safe environment where employees feel safe to discuss and report failures without fear of retribution. Such an environment encourages the surfacing of failures and fosters an open dialogue about why failures occurred and how they can be prevented in the future.

Moreover, Edmondson suggests that organizations need to move beyond superficial analyses of failures (such as blaming nonadherence to procedures) and adopt more sophisticated, context-specific strategies for learning. This might include using interdisciplinary teams to examine complex failures, thus gaining insights from multiple perspectives within the organization. This approach helps in understanding the root causes of failures and developing strategies that prevent future occurrences.

Edmondson's research emphasizes the crucial role of embracing risk-taking and failures as opportunities for growth. Her article details actionable strategies that organizations can implement to create a supportive environment that fosters continual learning and advancement.

## THINGS TO TRY

Building on Edmondson's suggestions for learning from failure, here are some things to do:

### Embrace and Learn from Failures

Shift your view of failure to see it as an essential part of development and innovation. Embrace failures from experimentation as crucial learning moments and treat every small misstep as a chance to improve. This mindset promotes perseverance and openness, encouraging you to explore new ideas fearlessly.

### Cultivate a Psychologically Safe Environment

Develop a setting where it's safe to discuss and learn from mistakes without fear of blame. This fosters an atmosphere that supports high performance and continuous innovation, enabling you and your team to openly analyze failures to foster growth and improvement.

### Promote Reflection and Cross-Disciplinary Learning

Regularly reflect on outcomes in order to refine your strategies and broaden your problem-solving skills through cross-disciplinary learning. Encourage structured experimentation to identify areas for improvement, which will enhance adaptability and innovation in your processes.

# Change of Outlook

Counterfactual analysis, also known as counterfactual thinking or "what if" analysis, is a cognitive process whereby individuals consider alternative outcomes or scenarios that could have occurred if past events had played out differently. In simpler terms, it involves imagining how things might have turned out if you had made different choices or if certain events had not happened.

Counterfactual analysis offers a powerful way to confront and manage the fear of failure. By exploring hypothetical situations, often used to assess the impact of specific decisions or events, you can speculate about alternative scenarios and possible outcomes. It can also be used to mentally revisit past decisions and events. For example, a painful breakup can serve as an opportunity to engage in self-reflection and analyze a current relationship. Perhaps the reason for the breakup was not what it had appeared to be. What if it was something else? And, are you repeating history unknowingly? Such counterfactual analysis might also be used to view a past event in a new light. Consider how the end of a job may have freed you up to start a new career that you had always hoped to pursue.

In this context, counterfactual analysis stands as a formidable weapon against the ever-looming human fear of failure. Here, you boldly confront your anxieties and uncertainties, transforming fear into a teachable moment that offers valuable lessons from past missteps and paves the way for a more resilient, informed, and confident approach to future challenges. This kind of analysis is a mental workout, an exercise in fortitude, and a compass guiding you through the complex terrain of your own choices and failure, imagined or otherwise.

Delve into the realm of "what if." Explore different paths that could have been taken, even those that might have led to failure. This exploration serves as a form of desensitization and normalization, gradually making you more comfortable with the idea of failure. By exposing yourself to the concept in a controlled, imaginative setting, you can diminish fear's grip on your decision-making.

Counterfactual analysis isn't about dwelling on past mistakes; it's about learning from them. Consider alternative choices and outcomes to gain valuable insights into the consequences of your actions. This learning process equips you to make more informed decisions in the future, reducing the likelihood of repeating past mistakes and the fear of encountering failure once again.

When you're confronted with new decisions or challenges, practice counterfactual thinking regularly. This mental exercise equips you to assess potential risks and rewards with greater confidence. Having mentally grappled with various scenarios, including those involving failure, you'll find that your decision-making abilities are enhanced.

Fear of failure often stems from regret over past decisions. Use counterfactual analysis to address and manage this regret actively. Explore alternative scenarios, recognizing that you believed that you made the best choice with the information available at the time. This realization can help alleviate the emotional burden associated with repeating failures of the past, allowing you to embrace some risk and move forward with greater clarity and resilience.

By incorporating counterfactual analysis into your life, you can transform fear into a catalyst for growth and self-improvement. Embrace the power of "what if" to navigate the uncertainties of life with courage and confidence.

# Apply the Paradoxical Mindset Cycle: We Attempt to Avoid Failure, but All Learning Is Developmental and Requires Failure

Reflect on your past experiences in which you failed in your endeavor.

### Step 1: Find the Paradox

**Question to Answer:** Where do I notice contradictions, inconsistencies, or illogical parts in my efforts to avoid failure despite knowing that failure is essential for learning and development?

**Things to Do:** Identify moments where actions, decisions, or feelings clash with the rest of the narrative. Look for elements that feel out of place or confusing.

### Step 2: Analyze the Meaning

**Question to Answer:** What underlying factors and insights can I uncover by examining from multiple perspectives and levels the paradox of avoiding failure while understanding its crucial role in the learning process?

**Things to Do:** Reflect on the facts and emotions to gain a deeper understanding of why the paradox exists and what it signifies.

## Step 3: Establish Guiding Principles

**Question to Answer:** What key learnings from my experiences with failure can be turned into guiding principles that will improve my effectiveness as a paradoxical thinker in future situations?

**Things to Do:** Reflect on the insights you've gained and identify specific aspects of those insights that can serve as actionable principles.

## Step 4: Implement Experiments

**Question to Answer:** What small, actionable changes can I implement based on my guiding principles to embrace failure as a vital part of the learning process and improve my growth?

**Things to Do:** Identify specific, manageable experiments; implement them; and reflect on their outcomes to refine your approach.

## PRACTICE THE FIRST PRINCIPLES: WE ATTEMPT TO AVOID FAILURE, BUT ALL LEARNING IS DEVELOPMENTAL AND REQUIRES FAILURE

### Abundance of Ideas

Embrace a variety of approaches and experiments, understanding that generating multiple solutions increases the likelihood of discovering what works, even through failure.

### Flexibility in Thinking

Adapt your mindset to see failure as a valuable part of the learning process, allowing you to pivot and adjust your strategies based on the lessons learned from setbacks.

## Risk-Taking

Take calculated risks and accept that failure is an inevitable and essential part of growth, enabling you to innovate and advance more effectively. Rather than avoiding failure, accelerate it. Engage in diverse experiments to quickly see what works and what doesn't, adjust the experiments for the next round, and repeat. Fail early, fail often, and fail off-Broadway.

## Curiosity

Cultivate a curious attitude toward failure, exploring the reasons behind it and seeking to understand how these insights can inform future successes.

## Perseverance

Persist in your efforts despite failures, recognizing that continual learning and improvement come from enduring through challenges and setbacks.

## Openness to Experience

Be open to new experiences and the possibility of failure, viewing them as opportunities for growth and development rather than as obstacles to be avoided.

## Self-Confidence

Build confidence in your ability to learn from failure, trusting that each setback is a stepping stone toward greater knowledge and eventual success.

## CHAPTER 8

# We Endeavor to Align the Change, but Change Is Driven by Deviance

I T ALL BEGAN WITH A pivotal gathering held in a spacious conference hall—a jumpstart event that brought together leaders, scientists, and key staff from a global pharmaceutical company. The objective was clear: to redesign the innovation processes in a large pharma to incorporate an agility found in a biotech start-up.

At the center of this transformative effort was Noor, the head of drug discovery, whose penchant for unconventional thinking and relentless exploration made her a driving force for change. Her unconventional nature was both a challenge and an asset. She constantly pushed and moved the boundaries of what was considered possible.

The two-day jumpstart event yielded a treasure trove of innovative ideas and potential therapies. The assembled group of experts carefully assessed the ideas in the context of the company's expertise, market positioning, and target areas for treatment. It was an exciting experience, filled with promise.

Unexpectedly, one of the company's owners, Gunter, joined the proceedings. His surprising encouragement sparked a reshuffling of priorities, resulting in the formation of smaller, specialized teams to delve deeper into the selected projects. Gunter offered his support before departing for Germany.

The ensuing discussions were intense, marked by debates about risk versus reward, traditional versus experimental approaches, and established versus emerging technologies. After three grueling days, the teams emerged with their proposals, physically and mentally exhausted but committed to their vision.

The climax arrived when Thomas, the senior VP of drug development, flew in from Europe to evaluate the ideas. His presence brought a sobering reality check. Thomas systematically disassembled the proposals, rejecting any notions of altering the organizational structure, creating shared workspaces, or investing in emerging technologies.

It became evident that a significant change in operational methods was required to realize our visionary therapies. A choice had to be made: maintain the existing efficiency, or embrace a more effective but unconventional approach.

Thomas, in a stern address, reinforced his position and his adherence to the directives issued by the board of directors. It was at this juncture that Noor, never one to shy away from challenging the status quo, reminded Thomas of Gunter's earlier support. Thomas, visibly embarrassed, adjourned the meeting and later chastised Noor in private.

The consequences were far-reaching. In the weeks that followed, Thomas made the drastic decision to terminate Noor's employment. Noor soon found herself in a similar role at a rival pharmaceutical firm, determined to advance two of the three proposed therapies.

The first therapy proved unfeasible early on and was abandoned. The second, marked by its innovative approach and technology, faced considerable challenges, but ultimately showed promise.

However, it was from these experiments, particularly the costly second one, that Noor derived critical insights. She developed a groundbreaking approach to drug discovery, ultimately yielding several highly successful drugs.

Meanwhile, the original pharmaceutical company continued to enjoy success, but found its growth constrained by limited markets for its existing product line. Thomas eventually retired, paving the way for a new senior VP to take over. In a twist, the new leader reached out to me for ideas on how to change the drug development organization. I told him to ask the few people remaining in the company who were part of the jump-start on the days that Gunter supported their work and Thomas didn't.

Opportunity walks in and out the door every day with the people who make things better and new. Noor's journey is a cautionary tale. It illustrates the delicate balance between aligning with established processes and embracing deviance to drive meaningful change. Successful change and innovation often require us to step outside the organizational structure to do the creative work the organization can't.

## A World of Imagination

In his essay "How Pixar Fosters Collective Creativity," Ed Catmull (2008), one of the masterminds behind Pixar, examines the innovative ethos driving Pixar's unparalleled success in animated storytelling. The studio, celebrated for pioneering films such as *Toy Story* and *Finding Nemo*, has changed the media industry with its trailblazing approach to both animation and the workplace. Central to its approach is a celebration of deviation from the norm, which acts as a catalyst for progress. Catmull emphasizes the vital role of open communication within Pixar's culture, in which hierarchical barriers have been dismantled to foster an environment of collaboration where ideas flow freely.

Crucially, Catmull highlights the necessity of creating a safe space for ideas to flourish. This environment, characterized by psychological safety, empowers individuals to contribute without fear of failure. Here, mistakes are seen as opportunities for growth rather than causes for reprimand, encouraging creative risk-taking and experimentation.

Leadership within Pixar's dynamic setting is multifaceted, extending beyond mere decision-making to establishing and promoting a culture of trust and collaboration. Catmull stresses the importance of leaders who actively engage in the creative process alongside their teams, fostering camaraderie and mutual respect. Through shared responsibility and continuous learning, teams forge bonds that drive them toward collective excellence.

At the heart of Pixar's creative engine lies the power of teamwork. Diverse talents converge to bring imaginative worlds to life. This collaborative synergy transcends barriers of language and geography, resulting in films that resonate globally. Pixar's example illustrates key principles for cultivating a workplace where creativity flourishes: open communication, psychological safety, and collaborative teamwork, which pave the way for boundless innovation and creative excellence.

## THINGS TO TRY

Ed Catmull suggests the following action steps to improve the creativity and effectiveness of your organization:

### Establish Open Communication Channels

Foster an inclusive environment where hierarchy takes a back seat to collaboration. Encourage open dialogue and idea sharing across all levels. Use such tools as anonymous suggestion boxes and regular meetings to gather diverse ideas, ensuring that everyone feels valued and heard.

### Empower and Support Team Members

Provide clear goals, but allow autonomy in approach. Foster a culture where risks are encouraged and failure is seen as a step to success. Support initiatives with the resources they need, fostering team members' confidence in pursuing ideas.

### Foster Learning and Adaptation

Reflect on project outcomes, focusing on learning and improvement. Use data analytics to track progress and inform decisions. View failures as opportunities for learning and growth, and encourage continual adaptation. Stanford psychologist Carol Dweck (2016) coins this the growth mindset in her book *Mindset: The New Psychology of Success*.

# Do as I Say, Not as I Do

I first crossed paths with Roger during an executive education course that I was leading on the intricate subjects of change and innovation leadership. He was a partner and a managing director of audit services at one of the world's largest accounting and management consultancies. A juggernaut in the accounting realm of financial audit, tax, legal advisory services, and business support, the firm had grown through decades of mergers and acquisitions.

Roger asked whether I would be willing to give a talk at a conference attended by board members from small-cap firms (firms with market capitalization between $250 million and $2 billion). One conversation led to another, and soon Roger was laying out the intricate challenge he was facing.

You see, Roger's consultancy had experienced its fair share of stumbles and setbacks, which had shaken public trust in the firm. But that wasn't even the crux of the issue. He pointed to a startling statistic: the number of publicly traded companies worth investing in had shrunk by nearly half over two decades. Private-equity firms had swept these once-public giants off the market, leading to decreased demand for financial audit, tax, and legal services from big accounting firms like Roger's.

Roger needed to transform his audit division, to be able to identify and work with these nimble and fast-growing small firms before they became giants. He needed his division to spot clients as a venture capital firm would but still function like an accounting powerhouse.

My team and I embarked on a comprehensive analysis of the accounting consultancy's strategy, market position, hiring practices, and more. The verdict was clear: They had to undergo a significant transformation if they were to capture these opportunities before their rivals did.

Our prescription was simple. We advised the firm to hire more young talent with technology backgrounds, the kind you'd typically find in engineering colleges. These recruits would need to visit incubators and tech showcases regularly. Moreover, the compensation structure for partners would have to be overhauled, as a new client could now drive revenue across various business sectors. The better a consultant was at landing a new high-growth client and the more services that client required from the firm, the greater the compensation the consultant would receive.

In essence, Roger had to convince his fellow senior partners to let him create a new subdivision that operated completely differently from the rest, one that didn't quite fit the existing operating or compensation models. The other partners, however, suggested that Roger consider pushing this new approach through a new type of service, which was decided in previous meetings and already underway—an innovation-and-technology line of services. The crux of the difference of the two approaches (a new subdivision versus a new service) is that the new service would be managed and operationalized as others, while the new subdivision would not. Even though the new division will still offer the same accounting services as before, in reality, it would have to be able to perform some practices that a venture capital firm would, with organizational structure, compensation model, practices, and culture that are considerably different from the rest of the company. It would introduce a radical change into the company, and that change might influence other changes in other divisions across the company. It definitely would bring a much bigger risk than a new service would.

I set up a meeting with Zola, the freshly appointed director of the innovation-and-technology service. Zola was eager and cooperative, but there was a catch. She had been tasked with developing the new service as an investment opportunity for the firm, essentially transforming it into a venture capitalist entity, taking equity stakes in emerging tech firms. This approach takes Roger's vision (identifying promising small firms) and more (investing in them), but keeps it in the existing operations. I tried to warn against this approach, emphasizing the extensive experience, capital, credibility, and vast networks required to succeed in the venture capital world. This approach seemed to be doing things in between the two pathways, not committing to one or the other. But my advice fell on deaf ears.

The irony was evident. Roger was determined to revamp the way his business operated to align it better with the company's overall goals, but he struggled to gain support from the managing partners. On the other hand, Zola aimed to establish a new line of business that operated like the existing ones, and she had the complete support of the managing partners. The key distinction was that Roger was altering the way the business functioned without changing its core focus. By contrast, Zola was shifting the core focus of the business while maintaining its traditional operational methods.

Both the audit and innovation-and-technology divisions struggled to achieve the growth Roger and Zola envisioned. They maintained their relative market positions—playing it safe, neither falling behind nor advancing.

Roger understood that genuine change demanded risk, investment, and the willingness to let go of the old to embrace the new. But he also learned that initiating something new was far simpler than dismantling the old, and far less effective when pursuing substantial transformation.

## Doing by Learning

Adopting a strategic approach is essential to effectively lead transformations while minimizing risks to the change leader. A pivotal aspect of doing so highlighted in "How to Integrate Work and Deepen Expertise" by Harvard professor Dorothy Leonard-Barton and colleagues (1994) is the necessity of maintaining a coherent vision throughout the development process. This vision acts as a guiding star, ensuring that all team members are aligned and that the project remains on course even when facing challenges. The article emphasizes that a well-articulated vision provides clarity, which is indispensable for driving change efficiently and with purpose.

Leadership in this context is not just about directing or managing resources but also about fostering an environment that encourages innovation and supports continuous learning. The article suggests that leaders should focus on cultivating their teams' capabilities incrementally and avoid the pitfalls of aiming for radical changes that might overwhelm and demotivate the teams. By nurturing a culture that values gradual improvement and detailed attention to the process, leaders can build a resilient organization capable of adapting to changes smoothly and effectively.

Moreover, the integration of functions within a project is fundamental for its success. Effective change leaders use strategies that facilitate cross-functional collaboration and integration. This involves breaking down silos and encouraging diverse departments to work together toward common goals. By leveraging various tools, leaders can enhance communication and collaboration across different teams, which is crucial for the seamless integration of complex projects.

Embracing out-of-the-box thinking is vital for organizations aiming to stay ahead in competitive markets. The article underscores the importance of challenging conventional wisdom and actively seeking innovative solutions that may lie outside traditional frameworks. This approach not only helps in overcoming existing rigidities within the organization but also paves the way for the development of new capabilities that can significantly boost the organization's competitive edge and responsiveness to market changes.

By using strategic approaches, change leaders can effectively manage transitions within their organizations while safeguarding their own roles and mitigating potential risks associated with change initiatives.

## THINGS TO TRY

In order to lead change initiatives while managing risks and promoting learning at the same time, follow these suggestions:

### Embrace Incremental Advances

Instead of overwhelming your development teams with the pressure to produce monumental achievements, focus on steady, incremental progress. This approach not only makes tasks more manageable but also facilitates sustained growth and improvement. For instance, setting smaller, achievable goals can lead to a cumulative effect that significantly propels development forward without the burnout associated with attempting massive leaps all at once.

## Value "Out-of-the-Box" Thinking

Challenge conventional wisdom by fostering an environment that encourages creative and innovative thinking. This can be achieved through methods such as innovative benchmarking, which involves using creative metrics to compare and measure performance against industry standards or competitors. In addition, tapping into the best minds in the field for fresh perspectives can provide invaluable insights that propel your organization ahead of the curve.

## Leverage Prototypes for Learning and Integration

Implement a practice of building a variety of prototypes early in the development process, which can significantly enhance learning and minimize errors. This approach allows teams to experiment and iterate quickly, thereby integrating various functions more cohesively. Moreover, regular prototyping can lead to a deeper understanding of the project requirements and potential pitfalls, ultimately leading to a more refined final product.

# Building Bridges

The paradox of managing change within organizations is often encapsulated in the effort to align diverse roles and perspectives within a unified strategy. Yet, as *Boston Scientific* cofounder John Abele (2011) suggests in his article "Bringing Minds Together," real transformation is frequently realized when we diverge from conventional paths and embrace deviance. This notion isn't about fostering disorder but about recognizing the value of diverse viewpoints and the innovative potential they bring. True progress has less to do with alignment and more to do with creating a tapestry of varied threads, each contributing uniquely to the broader vision.

In business environments where innovation is crucial, the integration of varied disciplines and perspectives can lead to breakthrough solutions that a homogenized approach might miss. Abele emphasizes the importance of interdisciplinary collaboration, through which distinct fields intersect to spark creativity and innovation. For instance, bringing together experts from unrelated disciplines can unearth unconventional solutions to complex problems. This collaborative approach not only enhances the solution space but also enriches the understanding across the board, promoting a culture where every perspective is valued and every voice has the potential to contribute meaningfully.

Challenging the status quo is another critical element in fostering a dynamic environment where change can truly occur. Encouraging team members to question established norms and explore uncharted territories requires a deliberate shift in organizational culture—one that rewards curiosity and courage over conformity. This mindset shift helps in dismantling the silos that often hinder collaborative efforts and stifle innovation. Leaders play a pivotal role here, not just by advocating for this approach but by embodying it, demonstrating that the path to innovative solutions often lies through unexplored terrains.

Lastly, integrating feedback from a broad range of stakeholders ensures that the initiatives are comprehensive and inclusive. Abele's discussion highlights how collaborative efforts can falter if there isn't genuine integration of feedback from all involved parties. This process is not merely about ticking a box but about actively engaging with different viewpoints to refine and improve outcomes. Each project, each dialogue, and each collaboration offers a learning opportunity, an occasion to better understand and harness the collective intelligence that drives substantial and meaningful change.

Through these approaches, organizations can shift from a rigid model of merely aligning change initiatives to a flexible model that truly drives change with the diverse and often deviant energies that characterize human creativity and ingenuity. This is the essence of mastering the paradoxes of change: leveraging the diverse to create a unified yet vibrant and innovative future.

## Apply the Paradoxical Mindset Cycle: We Endeavor to Align the Change, but Change Is Driven by Deviance

Reflect on a time in which you decided to go against the grain, rule, or procedure.

### Step 1: Find the Paradox

**Question to Answer:** Where do I notice contradictions, inconsistencies, or illogical parts in my efforts to align change within the organization while recognizing that true innovation often arises from deviance?

**Things to Do:** Identify moments where actions, decisions, or feelings clash with the rest of the narrative. Look for elements that feel out of place or confusing.

### Step 2: Analyze the Meaning

**Question to Answer:** What underlying factors and insights can I uncover by examining from multiple perspectives and levels the paradox of striving for alignment while embracing deviant ideas that drive meaningful change?

**Things to Do:** Reflect on the facts and emotions to gain a deeper understanding of why the paradox exists and what it signifies.

## Step 3: Establish Guiding Principles

**Question to Answer:** What key learnings from my experiences with both alignment and deviance can be turned into guiding principles to help me effectively manage and leverage these dynamics for innovation?

**Things to Do:** Reflect on the insights you've gained and identify specific aspects of those insights that can serve as actionable principles.

## Step 4: Implement Experiments

**Question to Answer:** What small, actionable changes can I implement based on my guiding principles to better balance alignment with the creative potential of deviant ideas, thus enhancing my ability to drive successful change?

**Things to Do:** Identify specific, manageable experiments; implement them; and reflect on their outcomes to refine your approach.

## PRACTICE THE FIRST PRINCIPLES: WE ENDEAVOR TO ALIGN THE CHANGE, BUT CHANGE IS DRIVEN BY DEVIANCE

### Abundance of Ideas

Embrace unconventional thinking and generate a multitude of diverse ideas, recognizing that deviance from the norm can lead to groundbreaking innovations.

### Flexibility in Thinking

Adapt your mindset to welcome and integrate deviant perspectives, understanding that flexibility in thought processes can harness the transformative power of diverse viewpoints. Accept that your plan may result in unintended consequences, and be ready to pivot.

## Risk-Taking

Take the bold step of supporting deviant ideas and approaches, knowing that true change often requires venturing into uncharted territory and challenging the status quo.

## Curiosity

Cultivate a curious mindset toward deviant ideas and practices, exploring how these unconventional methods can drive significant and meaningful change within your organization.

## Perseverance

Persist in advocating for and implementing deviant strategies, understanding that sustained effort is necessary to overcome resistance and achieve transformative change.

## Openness to Experience

Be open to new and deviant experiences, valuing the unique insights and opportunities they bring.

## Self-Confidence

Maintain confidence in your ability to lead and support deviant change initiatives, trusting that your belief in these unconventional methods will inspire others and foster successful outcomes.

# Conclusion

## Putting the Paradoxes to Work for You

W HAT IF THE ULTIMATE PARADOX of change is that there's no defin- itive "there" to arrive at? Consider the possibility that the true essence of change lies in your constantly engaging with the unfolding experience, adapting with grace to this shifting terrain. Your goal is not to reach a specific endpoint but to embrace the ongoing process of transformation. Think of this as a constant renewal, not an endless insta- bility. Holding this paradoxical mindset, you redefine success in terms of the depth of experiences gained and the flexibility of skills developed along the way.

Change and innovation often face resistance because there is no means of gathering data on the future where these efforts are manifested, and payoff is not guaranteed. This uncertainty can lead organizations to get stuck in the planning cycle—having meetings about meetings, writing reports about reports—without taking actionable steps forward. Fear of the unknown and the lack of concrete data can be paralyzing, which emphasizes the need for a mindset that embraces action despite uncertainty.

Consider the story of Benjamin Franklin. His life, marked by con- stant learning and evolution, encapsulates the essence of adaptability and the power of embracing one's incompleteness. Franklin's various roles—author, printer, inventor, scientist, statesman, diplomat, philanthropist, philosopher, and more—highlight his ability to embrace new challenges and continuously expand his horizons. He considered both his life and his country as works in progress, an insight that brings both a deep recognition of incompleteness as well as a powerful sense of destiny. His belief that they could be more, be better, pulled him ever onward.

As outlined in his autobiography, Franklin's (1790) *Plan for Attaining Moral Perfection* and the practice of his "Thirteen Virtues" illustrate a structured approach to self-improvement, which was revolutionary for its time and remains relevant today. Those virtues are temperance, silence, order, resolution, frugality, industry, sincerity, justice, moderation, cleanliness, tranquility, chastity, and humility.

Seeing his life as a continuous journey of learning and self-improvement allowed Franklin to remain open to new experiences and ideas, adapt to changing circumstances, and grow from each new challenge he faced. His autobiography, left unfinished, symbolizes this ongoing journey.

# Constant Transformation

Following the example of Franklin, we aim to create a system to perpetually generate growth for ourselves, much like a Van de Graaff generator. To do so, we need to put together several practices and approaches to use in our daily endeavor.

## Structuring Self-Improvement

Structured self-improvement is the foundation for personal and organizational growth. By adopting a disciplined approach to self-improvement, akin to Benjamin Franklin's Thirteen Virtues, you can systematically enhance your abilities and character. Start by identifying specific areas where you want to improve. These could be skills, behaviors, or attitudes that align with your personal values or professional goals. Create a set of clear, measurable goals and develop a plan to achieve them.

Implement regular self-assessment practices to track your progress. This could involve daily reflections, journaling, or seeking feedback from peers and mentors. The key is to remain committed to your goals, even when progress is slow or setbacks occur. This structured approach fosters a growth mindset, encouraging you to view challenges as opportunities for learning rather than as obstacles. By continuously refining your skills and behaviors, you set a positive example for those around you, inspiring them to embark on their own journeys of self-improvement.

This method helps you find and work through the paradoxes inherent in the journey of change. You may encounter conflicting priorities or values, but by systematically addressing them, you create a pathway to meaningful progress. Moreover, understanding that there's no final "there" to reach underscores the importance of ongoing self-improvement in navigating the continuous cycles of change.

## Embracing Incompleteness for Resilience

Embracing incompleteness means accepting that growth and development are ongoing processes. Instead of striving for perfection, recognize that both you and your organization are works in progress. This perspective fosters resilience by helping you remain adaptable and open to change. When you are faced with setbacks or unexpected challenges, viewing them as part of your ongoing journey rather than as final judgments enables you to respond with flexibility and creativity.

Cultivate a culture of continuous improvement within your organization by encouraging experimentation and learning from failures. Create an environment where feedback is welcomed and used constructively to drive growth. This approach not only builds individual resilience but also strengthens the collective ability of your team to navigate uncertainty and adapt to changing circumstances. By celebrating progress rather than perfection, you reinforce the value of perseverance and continuous effort.

By embracing the paradox of incompleteness, you acknowledge that although goals and milestones are important, the real value lies in the process and growth that occurs along the way. This mindset helps you and your organization become more resilient and more able to adapt to and thrive amid the continuous cycles of change.

## Acquiring Diverse Skills

Acquiring diverse skills is essential for thriving in a rapidly changing world. Following Franklin's example, actively seek out opportunities to broaden your skill set. Engage in activities and roles that push you beyond your comfort zone, enabling you to develop new competencies and perspectives. This might involve pursuing further education, taking on challenging projects, or collaborating with individuals from different backgrounds and disciplines.

Encourage a culture of lifelong learning within your organization by providing access to diverse learning opportunities and resources. Promote cross-functional collaboration and knowledge sharing, enabling team members to learn from one another's experiences and expertise. This not only enhances individual adaptability but also fosters a more innovative and resilient organization. By valuing and investing in yourself through learning diverse skills, you equip yourself and your team with the tools needed to navigate and thrive in an ever-evolving landscape.

This approach aligns with the paradoxical mindset, which accepts that there is no ultimate "there." Instead, the focus is on the continuous development of diverse skills to adapt and thrive. Engaging in varied learning experiences enables you to navigate the inherent paradoxes of change, such as balancing specialization with generalization, stability with flexibility. By acquiring diverse skills, you prepare yourself and your organization to effectively prosper in the continuous cycles of change.

# Incompleteness as Superpower

What if embracing our own limitations as leaders were the key catalyst for transformative growth within our organizations? The paradoxes of change, highlighted in the article "In Praise of the Incomplete Leader" by Deborah Ancona and her colleagues (2007), suggest that it's precisely our recognition of personal incompleteness that drives collective completeness. In that article, these thought leaders debunk the myth of the all-encompassing leader, advocating instead for a model where leaders acknowledge their own limitations and actively seek the diverse strengths of others to foster organizational change and growth.

Embracing incompleteness as a leader brings forth significant benefits, primarily through the cultivation of self-awareness that leads to collective strength. When leaders acknowledge their personal limitations, they open the door to embracing the collective intelligence and diverse skills of their team. Their act of humility and recognition paves the way for a more robust and inclusive approach to problem solving and innovation. It shifts the focus from individual capabilities to team strengths, fostering a synergistic environment where each member contributes their unique expertise.

Moreover, this acknowledgment of personal limitations is pivotal in fostering adaptability and resilience within the organization. Leaders who recognize their own limits in adaptability set a precedent for creating a culture where change is not merely tolerated but embraced. This attitude instills a sense of agility and readiness within the organization, making it better equipped to face new challenges and adapt to evolving circumstances.

Using your incompleteness as a superpower centers on embracing and leveraging your own limitations for the betterment of the organization. To do so, you need to take a real look at your strengths and weaknesses as a leader, team member, and family member, and at those around you.

## Conduct Honest Self-Evaluation and Foster Collaboration

Regularly assess your leadership skills and limitations. Acknowledging your weaknesses strategically optimizes your effectiveness and usefulness as both leader and team member. Use this self-awareness to identify where team members can complement your strengths and compensate for your weaknesses, promoting a well-rounded leadership approach through collaborative efforts.

The paradox here is that by admitting and embracing your limitations, you actually become a stronger leader. This honesty fosters trust and collaboration within your team, as members feel more valued and empowered to contribute their unique strengths. This ongoing process of self-evaluation and collaboration aligns with the continuous cycles of change, ensuring that both personal and organizational growth remain dynamic and adaptable.

## Champion Diverse Leadership and Align Goals

Actively advocate for diverse leadership representation to enrich decision-making with varied perspectives. Encourage the development of diverse leadership at all organizational levels. Ensure that your personal leadership goals align with collective objectives, amplifying team voices to pursue shared goals cohesively.

The paradox in diverse leadership is that by embracing a multitude of perspectives, which can often seem conflicting, you actually strengthen the decision-making process. By aligning your goals with the collective objectives, you navigate the inherent tensions between individual and team aspirations, creating a cohesive and adaptive organizational strategy. This approach recognizes that change is ongoing, and the diversity of thought and experience within your leadership team is a vital asset in navigating this continuous evolution.

## Cultivate Collaborative Culture and Continuous Learning

Create an environment where every team member feels valued and empowered to contribute their unique strengths. Foster collaboration through open forums, joint projects, and inclusive decision-making. Promote continuous learning and growth by embracing both successes and failures as opportunities for development, for both yourself and your team.

The paradox of collaboration and continuous learning lies in the balance between stability and innovation. While collaboration requires a stable environment where trust and open communication can flourish, continuous learning demands a willingness to challenge the status quo and embrace new ideas. By cultivating a culture that values both, you ensure that your organization remains adaptable and resilient in the face of ongoing change. This culture not only leverages individual and collective strengths but also turns every experience—whether a success or a failure—into a stepping stone for future growth.

# Tell a Different Story

Stories, like people, are works in progress—ever evolving and iterative. The paradox is that we tell these stories repeatedly until not only do we own the story, but the story comes to own us—it becomes an engine that encourages us to manifest our growth. By making small, iterative changes to our narratives, akin to revising a manuscript, we can transform ourselves. This process underscores that we are always writing and rewriting our story from within the story, continuously shaping and reshaping our identities and paths.

In their article "Storytelling That Drives Bold Change," Harvard business professor Frances Frei and entrepreneur Anne Morriss (2023) emphasize the transformative power of storytelling in effecting organizational change. They argue that a well-crafted narrative can significantly increase the odds of successful change implementation. The story a leader tells shapes their own attitude and molds the beliefs and attitudes of the entire organization. By articulating a vision in a clear and compelling manner, leaders can align their team's energy and direction toward meaningful change. This power of storytelling makes it a crucial tool in any change management strategy.

Furthermore, Frei and Morriss advocate for the dynamic nature of storytelling. Organizations and individuals can revisit and reinterpret past stories, altering the interpretation of the actions and actors involved. This reflective practice allows for the creation of new stories that offer insights and pathways to improved outcomes. It empowers leaders and teams to view past events through new lenses, which fosters a culture of continuous learning and adaptability.

This principle of storytelling is not confined to the business world; it also profoundly impacts our personal lives. By reevaluating the narratives we tell ourselves about our experiences and relationships, we can reshape our perceptions, foster personal growth, and steer our lives in new, more fulfilling directions.

Change is a constant in both the business world and our personal lives, but its success often hinges on how well change is communicated—how the story is told. Suppose you are at a pivotal point, needing to steer your organization—or your own life—through significant change. Here's how you can use storytelling as a powerful tool to drive this change effectively, leveraging both historical and forward-looking narratives to shape the future.

## Understand and Communicate Your Vision Clearly

Grasping the essence of the change you envision and articulating it clearly are foundational. Begin by thoroughly understanding the change, its implications, and its benefits. Communicate this vision in a way that resonates with your team, emphasizing both the necessity of the change and the opportunities it presents. Honor your organization's past achievements to create a bridge between the past and the future, showing how the new vision builds on previous successes.

Use clear, jargon-free language so that the vision is accessible to everyone, including you and your team. This clarity ensures that the message is not only understood but also embraced by all members of the organization. The story you tell about the future should be compelling, motivational, and aligned with the values and goals of your team. By effectively communicating your vision, you guide the team's energy and direction toward meaningful change.

## Develop a Data-Driven, Optimistic Strategy

An effective change strategy combines optimism with solid data. Outline a hopeful and detailed path forward, integrating selective data to bolster your narrative. This strategy should highlight the potential benefits of the change and provide concrete evidence to support the vision. By presenting data that underscores the need for change and the feasibility of the proposed path, you build credibility and confidence in the vision.

Employ diverse communication tools, such as digital media, photos, and vision boards, to make the message engaging for both you and your team. These tools can help visualize the future, making the abstract more tangible and relatable. By incorporating a variety of media, you cater to different learning styles and preferences, ensuring that the strategy resonates with a broader audience. This approach will help each member see how their efforts contribute to the collective goal, reinforcing their commitment to the change.

## Reinforce and Personalize the Change

Change is not a one-time event but a continuous process that requires constant reinforcement. Regularly reinforce the narrative of change across various platforms and meetings to embed it into the daily consciousness of both you and your team. This consistent messaging helps maintain momentum and keeps the vision at the forefront of everyone's mind.

Embrace and utilize emotions such as optimism and gratitude to deepen the connection to the vision, making it a personal mission for each team member, including yourself. Personalizing the change involves recognizing and celebrating individual contributions, fostering a sense of ownership and personal investment in the process. By tapping into positive emotions, you create a supportive and motivating environment that encourages everyone to stay engaged and committed to the change.

## Small Is Large

A fundamental paradox of knowledge is that we don't know what we don't know until we know it. Given that there is no data on the future where change is manifested, we need to diversify or hedge our actions. By taking smaller and wider steps, we acknowledge that failure is inevitable; we gain real information on what works and doesn't work, and we reduce risk because we have committed relatively little to each experiment. This approach is the opposite of the swaggering mantra "Go big or go home." People who go on crash diets, for example, seldom stay the course to their intended outcomes. Those who make gradual, sustainable changes to their eating habits and lifestyle are more likely to achieve and maintain their goals. This method provides valuable insights and learning opportunities, ensuring that our overall progress is steady and resilient, paving the way for sustainable, long-term success.

Changing your mindset is necessary but not enough on its own to make meaningful change happen. This requires taking action. Karl Weick's concept of "small wins" is a revolutionary approach that addresses the paradoxes of change, particularly in the context of organizational and social problems. In his article "Small Wins: Redefining the Scale of Social Problems," Weick (1984) argues that large, complex problems often overwhelm individuals and organizations, making it challenging to initiate and sustain meaningful change. However, by breaking down these issues into smaller, manageable parts—or small wins—individuals and organizations can tackle them more effectively. This strategy makes the process less daunting and creates a sense of achievement and momentum with each small victory. Incremental successes accumulate over time, leading to significant and lasting change. Weick's work is particularly insightful, as it shifts the focus from the enormity of problems to the empowering practicality of small, achievable steps, thus demystifying the complex process of change.

Weick provides some clues as to how to create the necessary momentum to start and perpetuate your transformational initiatives.

## Break Down a Large Task and Tackle It in Steps

Instead of feeling overwhelmed by a large task, break it down into smaller, manageable actions. To build confidence, start with tasks you can handle immediately. Each completed step boosts morale and propels you forward, demonstrating that significant change is achievable through incremental progress. This approach enables you to address paradoxes by managing complexity in a structured manner. Small, actionable steps make it easier to adapt and respond to new challenges as they arise, helping you maintain a clear focus on your ultimate goals without getting lost in the enormity of the task at hand.

## Celebrate Each Achievement

Take time to acknowledge and celebrate every small victory along the way. Recognizing these accomplishments reinforces your belief in your ability to drive change. Celebrations serve as milestones, reminding you of your progress and fueling your motivation to continue moving forward. Each celebration also acts as a reaffirmation of your commitment to the change process, making it easier to stay engaged and enthusiastic. This practice highlights the importance of appreciating the journey as much as the destination, turning each success into a stepping stone for the next phase of your transformational journey.

### Adapt and Stay Flexible

Anticipate changes as you make progress. Small wins may alter the landscape, requiring adjustments to your strategies. Stay agile and responsive, using each success as a learning opportunity. While focusing on small steps, keep the larger goal in sight, ensuring that every achievement contributes meaningfully to the overarching transformational journey. This flexibility allows you to navigate the inherent uncertainties and paradoxes of change, enabling you to pivot and refine your approach as needed. By remaining adaptable, you ensure that your efforts remain aligned with your evolving vision, making sustained progress possible even in the face of unforeseen challenges.

# Putting It All Together

It's time to integrate and apply the First Principles, paradoxes, and practices you've encountered in each chapter. This section is designed to help you consolidate your learnings and transform them into actionable strategies for personal growth and change. Through reflective exercises based on your stories, recognition of small wins, and application of the Paradoxical Mindset Cycle, you will gain a deeper understanding of your journey and equip yourself with practical tools for continuous development. This is the point where your acquired knowledge meets real-world application, empowering you to navigate life's complexities with greater awareness, resilience, and adaptability. Let's embark on this final, transformative phase of your journey with enthusiasm and an open mind, ready to harness the power of change for a more fulfilling and purposeful life.

Now let's take all your learnings and weave them into a cohesive plan. This plan will become your guide, one that will empower you to navigate the intricate maze of the paradoxes of change. Embrace the richness of your stories, the wisdom of your reflections, and the clarity of your strategies as you embark on this transformative path toward greater resilience and adaptability in the face of change.

As we bring all the chapters together, we will use the Paradoxical Mindset Cycle to harness the power of the paradoxes of change.

# Apply the Paradoxical Mindset Cycle: Putting the Paradoxes to Work for You

In this final chapter, you will take all your responses from throughout the book, identify overarching themes, integrate your guiding principles and experiments, and build them into a comprehensive plan. This plan will help you navigate future paradoxes with clarity and confidence.

## Step I: Find the Paradox

**Question to Answer:** Where do I notice contradictions, inconsistencies, or illogical parts in my stories that don't seem to fit or make sense?

**Things to Do:** Reflect on specific moments or experiences where your expectations clashed with reality. Identify situations where your efforts to implement change felt counterintuitive or resulted in unexpected outcomes.

### Developing Your Comprehensive Plan

A. *Review Your Stories*

- Go back through your previous stories and identify the paradoxes you have uncovered.

- Summarize each paradox in a few sentences.

B. *Identify Overarching Themes*

- Look for common themes or patterns across the paradoxes. These might include recurring behaviors, emotions, or situations.

- Note these themes, as they will help you understand the broader context of your paradoxes.

## Step 2: Analyze the Meaning

**Question to Answer:** What underlying factors and insights can I uncover by examining from multiple perspectives and levels the paradoxes I've encountered throughout my journey?

**Things to Do:** Dive deeper into the paradoxes you've identified. Consider different viewpoints and contexts to understand why these contradictions exist. Look for patterns and broader themes that offer insight into your experiences with change.

### Developing Your Comprehensive Plan

A. *Reflect on Underlying Factors*

- For each paradox, list the underlying factors that contribute to the paradox.
- Consider objective (factual), subjective (emotional), and symbolic (deeper meaning) perspectives.

B. *Synthesize Insights*

- Combine insights from different paradoxes to identify key learnings.
- Write down these insights, highlighting how they interconnect and influence your behavior and decision-making.

## Step 3: Establish Guiding Principles

**Question to Answer:** What key learnings from my entire experience with change can be turned into guiding principles that will improve my effectiveness as a paradoxical thinker in future situations?

**Things to Do:** Summarize the core lessons you've learned from dealing with paradoxes. Transform these lessons into guiding principles or rules of thumb that can help you navigate future changes more effectively.

### Developing Your Comprehensive Plan

A. *Formulate Guiding Principles*

- Based on the key learnings, create a set of guiding principles.
- Make sure that these principles are clear, actionable, and relevant to addressing the paradoxes you've identified.

B. *Integrate New Viewpoints*

- Think about how new viewpoints or behaviors can lead to different outcomes.
- Write down practical ways to apply these principles in various situations.

## Step 4: Implement Experiments

**Question to Answer:** What small, actionable changes based on my guiding principles can I implement to influence a broader context and enhance my paradoxical thinking, fostering continuous growth and adaptation?

**Things to Do:** Identify practical steps you can take to apply your guiding principles. Focus on small, manageable actions that can lead to significant improvements. Consider how these actions can impact not only your personal growth but also the broader environment around you.

### Developing Your Comprehensive Plan

A. *Design Experiments*

- For each guiding principle, design small experiments that you can easily implement.

- Ensure that these experiments are specific and achievable, and carry limited risk.

B. *Create an Action Plan*

- Develop a step-by-step action plan to implement these experiments.

- Include timelines, resources needed, and criteria for measuring success.

C. *Reflect and Adjust*

- After conducting each experiment, take time to reflect on the outcomes.

- Note what worked, what didn't, and what adjustments might be necessary.

- Use these reflections to refine your guiding principles and future experiments.

# Example of a Comprehensive Plan

In the introduction to this book, we started with an example story of an apple blossom tree that was cut down. Here we demonstrate how you would create a comprehensive plan from that story.

## Review Your Stories

- Paradox 1: Despite your love for trees and your creative problem-solving skills, you made an ill-advised decision to cut down the tree.

- Paradox 2: Despite typically being thoughtful and creative, you made a rushed and ill-considered decision due to stress and urgency.

- Paradox 3: Despite valuing thorough decision-making and consultation, you bypassed these steps in a moment of urgency.

- Paradox 4: Despite typically rushing to solve urgent issues, you took the time to explore options and consult other people, leading to a better outcome.

### Identify Overarching Themes

- Common themes: urgency, stress, and bypassing thorough decision-making

### Reflect on Underlying Factors

- Objective: quick decisions under stress
- Subjective: feeling of urgency and desire to resolve issues quickly
- Symbolic: need for control in unpredictable situations

### Synthesize Insights

- Key insight: In high-stress situations, the tendency to make quick decisions overrides your usual thorough decision-making processes.

### Formulate Guiding Principles

- Guiding principle 1: In urgent situations, pause and consult others before making a decision.
- Guiding principle 2: Allow time to explore multiple options before settling on a solution.

### Integrate New Viewpoints

- Viewpoint 1: Consulting other people, such as a significant other or partner, can generate different interpretations of the situation, meaningful insights, and alternative solutions.
- Viewpoint 2: Being pressured to be decisive brings about a manufactured sense of urgency that alters the perception of the situation.

## Design Experiments

- Experiment 1: In the next high-stress situation, take a five-minute break to gather your thoughts and consult with a trusted person.
- Experiment 2: When faced with an urgent decision, list at least three potential solutions and consider the pros and cons of each.

## Create an Action Plan

- Timeline: implementation of these experiments over the next month
- Resources: trusted person to consult; journal for recording options and reflections
- Success criteria: reduction in the number of regretful decisions; increased satisfaction with outcomes

## Reflect and Adjust

- After each experiment, write down what worked and what didn't.
- Adjust your guiding principles and experiments based on these reflections.

By following these steps and integrating your insights, guiding principles, and experiments into a comprehensive plan, you can enhance your paradoxical thinking and make more informed decisions in future situations.

# Onward, Ever Onward!

As you move forward from this point, do so with the knowledge that your journey through change is an active, ongoing process. The tolerance of ambiguity you've developed is a powerful tool. It enables you to navigate the complexities of change with a clear head and a steady hand. Embracing uncertainty isn't about having all the answers; it's about being comfortable in the space where questions exist. This tolerance is your strength, a quiet acknowledgment that not all paths are straight or clear, yet all are traversable.

Your paradoxical mindset is your compass in this journey. It's a mindset that doesn't just react to change but anticipates and engages with it proactively. Remember, adaptability is about flexibility in thought and action. It's about being open to new ideas, willing to adjust plans, and ready to embrace new ways of thinking. This mindset doesn't promise a smooth journey, but it does equip you to handle the twists and turns with agility and insight.

As you advance onward, let these insights guide you. Each step, whether tentative or confident, is a part of a larger journey of growth and impact. In this journey, you're not just a passive observer; you're an active participant, shaping your path with each decision and action.

Proceed with the assurance that your journey is as unique as your fingerprints—distinctly yours. It's a journey marked not by grand gestures but by thoughtful steps, each one a testament to your commitment to personal and professional growth. Venture onward with the knowledge that every challenge is an opportunity to learn, and every success, a chance to reflect and refine. Your journey through the paradoxes of change is not just about reaching a destination; it's about building wisdom and resilience along the way.

# THE ART OF CHANGE
## DISCUSSION GUIDE

I N *THE ART OF CHANGE,* authors Jeff DeGraff and Staney DeGraff explore the intricate dynamics of personal and organizational transformation through the lens of paradoxes inherent in the change process. This discussion guide is designed to delve into each chapter of the book, prompting readers who are studying change and innovation to reflect deeply on their own experiences and the theoretical concepts presented. By examining the Paradoxical Mindset Cycle, the challenges of changing others, the limitations within oneself, the role of facts in persuasion, the evolving nature of goals, the productive aspects of conflict, the educational value of failure, and the unconventional paths driven by deviance, readers are encouraged to think critically and engage in meaningful dialogue. These discussions aim to equip readers with a robust understanding of how change can be effectively managed and harnessed for personal growth and innovation, providing a structured yet flexible framework for exploring the paradoxes of change.

## Facilitator Guide: Creating an Active, Productive, and Positive Discussion

To lead an effective discussion that engages readers and encourages them to apply the key ideas of *The Art of Change* to their own lives and workplace situations, it's essential to foster an environment that values open communication, reflection, and practical application. Begin by setting clear objectives for the discussion, emphasizing the importance of connecting theoretical concepts from the book to personal experiences and current events. Encourage readers to share their thoughts and stories, ensuring that their contributions are validated in order to create an atmosphere of trust and inclusivity.

Introduce a variety of interactive discussion techniques such as small-group breakouts, role playing, or case studies that mirror real-life scenarios readers might encounter in their careers or experience. These methods help contextualize the paradoxes discussed in the book, making them more tangible and relatable. Pose open-ended questions that challenge readers to think critically about how they can implement the lessons they learned in various situations, particularly in those involving change and conflict.

Incorporate reflective practices such as journaling or peer-to-peer feedback sessions, enabling readers to internalize the concepts and explore their implications in a deeper, more personal way. In addition, ensure that the space is a safe and supportive environment by establishing ground rules that promote respectful listening and encourage open sharing without fear of judgment or criticism. Emphasize confidentiality, the value of diverse perspectives, and positive reinforcement. Make sure that they feel that their contributions are acknowledged and appreciated, creating an inclusive climate. By ensuring that the space is a safe one and facilitating a dynamic learning environment, you can help readers not only grasp but also apply the transformative insights from the book to become more adaptive and innovative thinkers in their personal and professional journeys.

## Introduction

In the introduction, "Inviting Paradox In," the authors set the stage for embracing the complex and often contradictory nature of change. This guide invites participants to consider the foundational concept of paradoxes and their significance in understanding and navigating change. The discussion points encourage a reflective exploration of initial impressions about paradoxes and set expectations for the transformative insights to be gained throughout the book.

### Key Question

- How can embracing paradoxes rather than resisting them be beneficial in the context of change?

### Discussion Points

- Reflect on a recent global or local event where a paradox was clearly at play. How did this paradox impact the outcomes?
- Discuss how your understanding of paradoxes could influence your approach to upcoming changes in your personal and professional journeys.

## Chapter 1

Chapter 1, "The Paradoxical Mindset Cycle," introduces a systematic approach to cultivating adaptability through reflecting, analyzing, and owning personal narratives. This discussion will focus on the practical steps of the Paradoxical Mindset Cycle, emphasizing the importance of personal reflection and pattern recognition in fostering an adaptive approach to life's challenges and changes.

### Key Question

- What steps are involved in the Paradoxical Mindset Cycle, and how can they be applied to personal growth?

### Discussion Points

- Share a personal story where adapting to a change significantly altered your perspective or outcome. What stages of the Paradoxical Mindset Cycle can you identify in your story?
- How can the Paradoxical Mindset Cycle be applied to current global challenges such as climate change or social inequality?

## Chapter 2

In chapter 2, "We Seek to Change Others, but Can Only Change Ourselves," the authors challenge the common impulse to alter others' behaviors instead of focusing on self-change. The discussion explores the dynamics of influence and personal development, probing the efficacy and outcomes of attempts to change others versus transforming oneself.

*Key Question*

- Why is focusing on changing oneself more effective than attempting to change others?

*Discussion Points*

- Recall a situation where you attempted to change someone else's opinion or behavior. What were the results, and what did you learn about your own capacities for change?
- How can this principle be applied in a leadership or teamwork setting, especially in diverse environments?

## Chapter 3

Chapter 3, "We Aspire to Transcend Our Own Limits, but Must Do So from within Them," examines the paradox of personal limits and the aspiration to exceed them. This section encourages an examination of the balance between acknowledging limitations and leveraging them as catalysts for growth and transcendence.

*Key Question*

- How can recognizing and embracing one's limits lead to personal and professional growth?

*Discussion Points*

- Discuss a time when acknowledging a personal limitation opened up new opportunities for growth or innovation.
- How can you be sure what your limitations are?

## Chapter 4

In chapter 4, "We Use Facts to Change Minds, but Minds Aren't Changed by Facts," the discussion pivots to the limitations of factual arguments in changing beliefs. Readers will analyze the interplay between rational data and emotional or belief-based responses, exploring more effective ways to persuade and influence through understanding themselves and others.

*Key Question*

- Why might facts alone be insufficient to change someone's beliefs or attitudes?

*Discussion Points*

- Can you think of a public figure or a media event where facts failed to persuade the public? Discuss the role of narrative and emotion in these cases.
- In your experience, how have you seen beliefs or biases resist factual arguments? How did you or others attempt to address this challenge?

## Chapter 5

Chapter 5, "We Set Goals for Change, but the Goals Change with the Change," discusses the fluid nature of goals in the context of ongoing change. The conversation will center on strategies for setting adaptable goals and the necessity of flexibility in planning to accommodate evolving circumstances and insights.

*Key Question*

- How can we adapt our goals flexibly in response to changing circumstances?

*Discussion Points*

- Describe a personal or professional goal that evolved over time due to changing circumstances. What did you learn from this experience?
- How can this principle of flexible goal-setting be useful in uncertain times, such as during the current economic or health crises?

## Chapter 6

In chapter 6, "We Try to Minimize Conflict, but Change Is Created by It," the authors posit that conflict, often avoided, is a potent catalyst for change. This section examines how conflict can be constructively harnessed to foster innovation and growth, challenging readers to rethink their approaches to conflict in change scenarios.

*Key Question*

- How can conflict be a catalyst for change rather than a barrier?

*Discussion Points*

- Share a case from your life or a historical event where conflict led to positive change. What were the key factors that transformed conflict into a catalyst?
- Discuss how understanding this paradox can help when working in teams or in other organizational units.

## Chapter 7

Chapter 7, "We Attempt to Avoid Failure, but All Learning Is Developmental and Requires Failure," shifts focus to the role of failure in learning and development. Discussions will explore the concept of "productive failure" and how embracing failure as a fundamental component of learning can enhance personal and professional development.

### Key Question

- Why is embracing failure crucial for learning and development?

### Discussion Points

- Think of a personal failure that turned out to be a valuable learning experience. What did you learn, and how did it help you grow?
- How can your organization incorporate this understanding of failure to improve personal and professional growth?

## Chapter 8

Chapter 8, "We Endeavor to Align the Change, but Change Is Driven by Deviance," explores the tension between seeking alignment in change efforts and the disruptive nature of deviance, which often drives significant change. This section will provoke thoughts on the balance between conformity and deviation in effecting meaningful change.

### Key Question:

- Why might standard methods of implementing change not always be effective?

### Discussion Points

- Provide an example from your experience or a well-known case where deviating from the norm led to significant breakthroughs or improvements.
- How can fostering a culture that embraces deviance lead to innovation in personal or professional settings?

## Conclusion

The conclusion wraps up the discussions with a synthesis of the key lessons and insights gained from delving into each paradox. This final part of the discussion guide aims to consolidate understanding and inspire readers to apply these insights in their ongoing personal and professional journeys in change and innovation.

### *Key Question*

- What are the key takeaways from the book regarding managing and understanding change?

### *Discussion Points*

- How will you apply the insights from this book to your future career or personal life?
- Discuss how these paradoxes of change could be integrated into corporate training programs to better prepare all team members and the company for future challenges.

# REFERENCES

Abele, J. (2011, July/August). Bringing minds together. *Harvard Business Review*, *89*(7–8), 86–93.

Ancona, D., Malone, T. W., Orlikowski, J., & Senge, P. M. (2007, February). In praise of the incomplete leader. *Harvard Business Review, 85*(2), 92–100.

Beckman, S. L., & Barry, M. (2007). Innovation as a learning process: Embedding design thinking. *California Management Review, 50*(1), 25–56. https://doi.org/10.2307/41166415

Cameron, K. (1986). Effectiveness as a paradox: Consensus and conflict in the conceptions of organizational effectiveness. *Management Science, 32*(5), 539–553.

Carse, J. (2011). *Finite and infinite games*. Free Press.

Catmull, E. (2008). How Pixar fosters collective creativity. *Harvard Business Review, 86*(9), 64–72.

Davenport, T. H. (2009, February). How to design smart business experiments. *Harvard Business Review, 87*(2), 68–76.

DeGraff, J. T. (2015, March 9). You can't predict the future. But here's what you can do. *Inc.* https://www.inc.com/jeff-degraff/the-future-has-come-and-gone-you-just-missed-it.html

DeGraff, J. T., & DeGraff, S. (2017). *The innovation code: The creative power of constructive conflict*. Berrett-Koehler.

Dewey, J. (1910). *How we think*. D. C. Heath.

Dewey, J. (1916). *Democracy and education: An introduction to the philosophy of education*. Macmillan.

Dweck, C. (2016). *Mindset: The new psychology of success*. Ballantine Books.

Edmondson, A. C. (2011, April). Strategies for learning from failure. *Harvard Business Review, 89*(4), 48–55.

Eisenhardt, K. M., & Sull, D. (2001, January). Strategy as simple rules. *Harvard Business Review, 79*(1), 106–116.

Follett, M. P. (1924). *Creative experience*. Longmans, Green and Co.

Franklin, B. (1790). *Plan for attaining moral perfection*. https://resources.finalsite.net/images/v1585159253/rentonschoolsus/fjwu7ezjt5fkqo8t09kq/IBLASL2B-TextA-MoralPerfection.pdf

# References

Frei, F., & Morriss, A. (2023, November-December). Storytelling that drives bold change. *Harvard Business Review, 101*(6), 62–71.

Kolbert, E. (2017, February 20). Why facts don't change our minds. *New Yorker.* https://www.newyorker.com/magazine/2017/02/27/why-facts-dont-change-our-minds

Kross, E. (2021). *Chatter: The voice in our head, why it matters, and how to harness it.* Random House.

Leonard, D., & Swap, W. (2005). *Deep smarts: How to cultivate and transfer business wisdom.* Harvard Business School Press.

Leonard-Barton, D., Bowen, H. K., Clark, K. B., Holloway, C., & Wheelwright, S. C. (1994, September/October). How to integrate work and deepen expertise. *Harvard Business Review, 72*(5), 121–130.

McGrath, R. G. (2010). *Discovery-driven growth: A breakthrough process to reduce risk and seize opportunity.* Harvard Business School Press.

Merriam-Webster. (n.d.) Paradox. In *Merriam-Webster.com dictionary.* Retrieved July 12, 2024, from https://www.merriam-webster.com/dictionary/paradox

Mintzberg, H. (1994). *The rise and fall of strategic planning.* Free Press.

Quinn, R. E. (2005, July-August). Moments of greatness: Entering the fundamental state of leadership. *Harvard Business Review, 83*(7), 74–83.

Rosch, E. (2008). Beginner's mind: Paths to the wisdom that is not learned. In M. Ferrari & G. Potworowski (Eds.), *Teaching for wisdom* (pp. 135–162). Springer. https://doi.org/10.1007/978-1-4020-6532-3_8

Torrance, E. P. (1974). *Torrance tests of creative thinking.* Scholastic Testing Service.

Torrance, E. P. (1987). Teaching for creativity. In S. G. Isaksen (Ed.), *Frontiers of creativity research: Beyond the basics* (pp. 189–215). Bearly Limited.

Weick, K. E. (1984). Small wins: Redefining the scale of social problems. *American Psychologist, 39*(1), 40–49. https://doi.org/10.1037/0003-066X.39.1.40

Weick, K. E. (2000). *Making sense of the organization.* Blackwell Publishers.

Whitehead, A. N. (1929). *Process and reality.* Macmillan.

Wilson, E. O. (2017). *The origins of creativity.* Liveright.

# ACKNOWLEDGMENTS

W E CONVEY OUR SINCERE GRATITUDE to everyone who has turned this endeavor into reality, including our Innovatrium team: John DeGraff, Sarah Hussong, Bridget Bunnay, Celeste Dryjanski, Melissa "Cleo" Smith, Ethan Eagle, Johnny Barnes, Kelley "Crash" Sawyer, Maggie Chen, and Crystal Bean, who have undertaken more responsibilities and managed more things to give us time to work on this book. A special thank you to Logan Scherer, who makes music with his words.

Thank you to our extended family of experts—Darren Schumacher, Atul Dhir, and Joe Byrum—who have kept us learning, stretching, and growing. They always make this journey fun.

To our Berrett-Koehler team: Steve Piersanti, Jeevan Sivasubramaniam, Christy Kirk and her marketing team, and Katelyn Keating and her production team, we thank you for bringing this book to life and making it great.

We are especially grateful to our reviewers: Deborah Nikkel, Ellyn Kerr, and Jackie Stavros. Your comments and advice have been very helpful.

This book would probably not have materialized without countless conversations with many of our corporate and military clients. They are the heart of this book. Thank you for all the stories, experiences, and trust.

# INDEX

# ABOUT THE AUTHORS

**Jeff DeGraff** has been a professor of management and organization at the Ross School of Business at the University of Michigan for thirty-five years. He cofounded the Innovatrium, a boutique consulting firm, to complete his mission to *democratize innovation*. Called the "Dean of Innovation" because of his expertise, Jeff has consulted with more than half of the Fortune 500 companies in various industries and countries, art organizations, and governmental entities. He received his PhD from the University of Wisconsin when he was twenty-five years old.

**Staney DeGraff** is the CEO of Innovatrium, a small consulting firm in the heart of the University of Michigan central campus. Her research interests address the concept of constructive conflict and the measures of innovation. She is now busy conducting her research on cognitive mobility/adaptability and human performance. She has an MBA and an MSE in computer engineering from the University of Michigan.

Jeff and Staney live in Ann Arbor and have three children and one grandson, and, they hope, will have some Shelties in the near future.

Also by Jeff DeGraff and Staney DeGraff

# The Innovation Code
## The Creative Power of Constructive Conflict

In *The Innovation Code*, Jeff DeGraff, dubbed the "Dean of Innovation," and Staney DeGraff introduce a simple framework to explain the ways different kinds of thinkers and leaders can create constructive conflict in any organization. Drawing on their work with nearly half of the Fortune 500 companies, the DeGraffs give you tools and methods to harness the creative energy that arises from opposing viewpoints. This positive tension produces ingenious solutions that go far beyond "the best of both worlds." Using vivid examples, *The Innovation Code* offers four steps to normalize conflict and channel it to develop something completely new. By following these simple steps, you will get breakthrough innovations that are good for both you and your customers.

Hardcover, ISBN 978-1-5230-8476-0
PDF ebook, ISBN 978-1-5230-8477-7
ePub ebook, ISBN 978-1-5230-8478-4

BK Berrett–Koehler Publishers, Inc.
*www.bkconnection.com*                    **800.929.2929**

# The Innovation Code Card Game
## The Creative Power of Constructive Conflict

This companion game to *The Innovation Code* brings leadership training to life in a new way. Get your leaders and employees up and moving, discovering their strengths and passions in an interactive, fully immersive game.

The Competing Values Card Deck is a great, immersive experience for organizations. The card deck helps teams sort themselves into the quadrants of the Innovation Code model, and then participants use the included and ancillary materials to learn more about their teams. Armed with this knowledge, teams will be able to leverage the concepts of competition and collaboration in their organizations. Get ready to get a whole room of people up, moving around, and talking to each other without resorting to questions about everyone's favorite ice cream flavor.

Cards, ISBN 978-1-5230-9434-9

Berrett–Koehler Publishers, Inc.
*www.bkconnection.com*          **800.929.2929**

# The Creative Mindset
## Mastering the Six Skills That Empower Innovation

Nearly all of today's major innovation workshops and programs call on organizations to drive innovation. What they miss is that innovation comes from the personal creativity of individuals. And creativity doesn't require an advanced education or technical skills—all employees can be creative. Often, all they lack is a fitting mindset and the right tools.

*The Creative Mindset* brings how-to advice, tools, and techniques from two master innovators who have taught and worked with over half of all the Fortune 500 companies. Jeff and Staney DeGraff introduce six essential creative-thinking skills that can be easily mastered with limited practice and remembered as the acronym CREATE: Concentrate, Replicate, Elaborate, Associate, Translate, and Evaluate. These six skills, sequenced as steps, simplify and summarize the most important research on creative thinking and draw on over thirty years of real-world application in some of the most innovative organizations in the world. It's time to rethink the way we make innovation happen. As the spirit of Chef Gusteau proclaims in the Pixar classic *Ratatouille*, "Anyone can cook."

Paperback, ISBN 978-1-5230-9015-0
PDF ebook, ISBN 978-1-5230-9016-7
ePub ebook, ISBN 978-1-5230-9017-4

BK® Berrett–Koehler Publishers, Inc.
*www.bkconnection.com*                    800.929.2929

# Introducing the Berrett-Koehler Community

**Support mission-based publishing while saving up to
30 percent on all books and attending exclusive events**

Are you passionate about supporting independent
publishing and reading diverse voices and
perspectives?

Join the BK Community Membership Program and
become a part of a vibrant literary community.
Since 1992 we have been discovering and
amplifying the voices of authors who drive positive
change through books that connect people and
ideas to create a world that works for all.

This membership program will help Berrett-Koehler
Publishers thrive financially, broaden and deepen
our global community, spread our mission, and
diversify our revenues for a sustainable future.

Visit ideas.bkconnection.com/bkcommunity-join or scan the QR code
to learn more and become a member.

## Berrett–Koehler
### Publishers

**Berrett-Koehler** is an independent publisher dedicated to an ambitious mission: *Connecting people and ideas to create a world that works for all.*

Our publications span many formats, including print, digital, audio, and video. We also offer online resources, training, and gatherings. And we will continue expanding our products and services to advance our mission.

We believe that the solutions to the world's problems will come from all of us, working at all levels: in our society, in our organizations, and in our own lives. Our publications and resources offer pathways to creating a more just, equitable, and sustainable society. They help people make their organizations more humane, democratic, diverse, and effective (and we don't think there's any contradiction there). And they guide people in creating positive change in their own lives and aligning their personal practices with their aspirations for a better world.

And we strive to practice what we preach through what we call "The BK Way." At the core of this approach is *stewardship,* a deep sense of responsibility to administer the company for the benefit of all of our stakeholder groups, including authors, customers, employees, investors, service providers, sales partners, and the communities and environment around us. Everything we do is built around stewardship and our other core values of *quality, partnership, inclusion, and sustainability.*

We are grateful to our readers, authors, and other friends who are supporting our mission. We ask you to share with us examples of how BK publications and resources are making a difference in your lives, organizations, and communities at bkconnection.com/impact.

Dear reader,

Thank you for picking up this book and welcome to the worldwide BK community! You're joining a special group of people who have come together to create positive change in their lives, organizations, and communities.

## What's BK all about?

Our mission is to connect people and ideas to create a world that works for all.

Why? Our communities, organizations, and lives get bogged down by old paradigms of self-interest, exclusion, hierarchy, and privilege. But we believe that can change. That's why we seek the leading experts on these challenges—and share their actionable ideas with you.

## A welcome gift

To help you get started, we'd like to offer you a **free copy** of one of our bestselling ebooks:

### bkconnection.com/welcome

When you claim your **free ebook**, you'll also be subscribed to our blog.

## Our freshest insights

Access the best new tools and ideas for leaders at all levels on our blog at ideas.bkconnection.com.

Sincerely,

Your friends at Berrett-Koehler